"*Move On Motherf*cker* (MOMF) is a modern, efficacious self-help tool kit designed to provide relief for people with common mental health issues surrounding depression, anxiety, low self-esteem, bad habits, and personal or work-related relationship problems. Readers will discover how to change and improve problematic behavior patterns and negative thoughts through a series of compelling vignettes, exercises, and self-reflections without getting lost in the weeds of therapeutic psychobabble. It's a 'hell-yes,' hands-on, user-friendly approach to begin feeling empowered to get better."

—**Timothy Jay, PhD**, professor of psychology emeritus at
Massachusetts College of Liberal Arts, and author of *Why We Curse*

"Honest, salty self-talk can be a true balm for anxiety, shame, sadness, and despair. So take it from one motherf*cker to another: move on, and read this book!"

—**Sarah Knight**, *New York Times* bestselling author of
Calm the F*ck Down

"MOMF is like that blunt friend who calls you on your sh*t and puts things into f*cking perspective. Using humor, *a lot* of profanity, and the foundation of cognitive behavior therapy (CBT), Eckleberry-Hunt's book guides readers through a reality check, and teaches them to change the voice of negativity and doubt to that of a motherf*cker who is ready to kick ass! This is a reader's guide to self-empowerment!"

—**Britt A. Nielsen, PsyD, ABPP**, associate professor of psychiatry
and psychology at The MetroHealth System and Case Western
Reserve University

"I enthusiastically recommend MOMF to my patients, colleagues, friends, and family. This book is an incredible tool, incorporating humor, honesty, and a little rebelliousness on the journey to become the best version of ourselves. The vignettes, reflections, and activities are relevant and empowering. Using MOMF, you will laugh, learn, and hopefu

—**Lori Wa** ler Private Physicians in
Troy, M enty years; and clinical
faculty : am Beaumont Medical School

D1403028

"If you are searching for help living your best life, this book is for you! MOMF teaches you how to use profanity and humor to move past negative self-talk toward reaching your goals and finding peace and happiness. MOMF is the friend that gives it to you straight and urges you to move forward. There isn't a friend, family member, or patient of mine that couldn't benefit from reading this."

—**Jennifer Tucciarone, MD**, family medicine physician

"In a sea of self-help books, it is understandable to ask, 'why this one?' Simply put, this is *the* book to get if you are finally ready to change your life. You will get straight talk about how to move on and begin truly living your life today. Written in an engaging and humorous style, this book delivers. I will be strongly recommending this book to my patients."

—**Darren R. Jones, PhD, LP**, director of behavioral medicine clinical operations, and director of resident wellness at Beaumont Health

MOVE ON MOTHERF*CKER

LIVE, LAUGH &
LET SH*T GO

JODIE ECKLEBERRY-HUNT, PhD

New Harbinger Publications, Inc.

Publisher's Note

This publication is designed to provide accurate and authoritative information in regard to the subject matter covered. It is sold with the understanding that the publisher is not engaged in rendering psychological, financial, legal, or other professional services. If expert assistance or counseling is needed, the services of a competent professional should be sought.

Distributed in Canada by Raincoast Books

Copyright © 2020 by Jodie Eckleberry-Hunt
New Harbinger Publications, Inc.
5674 Shattuck Avenue
Oakland, CA 94609
www.newharbinger.com

Cover design by Amy Shoup

Acquired by Jennye Garibaldi

Edited by Marisa Solis

All Rights Reserved

FSC
www.fsc.org
MIX
Paper from
responsible sources
FSC® C011935

Library of Congress Cataloging-in-Publication Data on file

Printed in the United States of America

22   21   20

10   9   8   7   6   5   4   3   2   1   First Printing

Contents

Foreword

I've dabbled in self-help books in the past. I've tried journaling and mindfulness. But I've always had the sneaking suspicion that the authors of these books wanted me to be a more saintly, more grace-filled, more infinitely patient version of myself. This book, in contrast, knows that I'm sometimes a motherfucker, who just can't get out of her own damned way. If that sounds like you, then dive in.

Jodie Eckleberry-Hunt has written a manifesto and manual for the imperfect, impatient, and impertinent among us. She blends tried-and-true techniques from her years of clinical practice with the latest cutting-edge research on the benefits of being salty. And also, it's fucking *funny!*

There are benefits aplenty to salty language. In my own research on swearing, I discovered that people are more likely to use strong language to sympathize, to amuse, or to express frustration than they are to use it abusively. Sure, there are some assholes out there, but most of us mofos just use cussing to get through the inevitable frustrations of living in the real world.

Research also shows that swearing really does help with pain—whether it's the emotional kick-in-the-nuts of a bad breakup, or an actual kick in the actual nuts. Swearing lessens pain's hold over us and lets us find new reserves of strength. Swearing seems to go back as far as humanity; some of the earliest recorded informal writing (call it the Roman equivalent of scribbling in a toilet stall) has plenty of rude, ribald, and robust language. And even chimpanzees, when taught to sign, invent a swearing lexicon as soon as they internalize their first taboo.

While you're not likely to find swearing in psychology textbooks (yet), there's plenty of data to show that it's a tool we need in our language. It's a form of language so pervasive and profound that it can even withstand the kind of brain damage that robs us of the ability to use any other words.

Dr. Eckleberry-Hunt has figured out a way to make the power of swearing work for you. So say "fuck yeah" to the possibility of facing that pain, releasing that frustration, and dealing with the assholes getting in your way—even when one of those assholes is you.

It's time to embrace the power of MOMF.

—Emma Byrne, PhD
author of *Swearing Is Good for You*

#*@&*!!

Introduction

Like a lot of ideas that work, what I am going to teach you started with a personal disaster.

Here's the story of how "move on, motherfucker" was born.

I've been a health psychologist for nearly two decades now. I love the work, *love* it. But does that mean I always love my job? No, it does not.

In addition to my private practice, I work with hospitals and medical schools, teaching doctors and medical students to help people with psychological and emotional concerns. After eleven enjoyable years with a great organization, I found a new job closer to home.

This, as it turned out, was a mistake.

I arrived at the new place full of ideas and enthusiasm. But I quickly discovered it was really dysfunctional. Even chaotic. Soon I was obsessing about what a terrible decision I'd made changing jobs. This was not helpful, but I could not seem to stop.

In my therapy practice, I help patients try to focus on what they can control: themselves. Clearly, it was time to practice what I'd preached. So I told myself to let go of trying to fix everything that was messed up. I told myself to stop taking on more responsibility in order to make it better. I told myself to ignore the negativity that surrounded me. I told myself to let go of the urge to change things that I couldn't control. I told myself to stop being so perfectionistic and controlling. I told myself to just breathe and let go.

My self replied, "Fuck you!"

And I went back to freaking out.

So I was really doomed, right? None of my therapist techniques were doing what I needed them to: give me some relief, get me out of my rut, help me face another day with some level of peace.

Feeling helpless, I started cursing *a lot.* In my car, in my office, at my emails, in bathroom stalls, under my breath. It was a way to cope. One like-minded colleague and I started having cursing contests, one-downing each other until we'd burst out laughing. It did make us feel better for a few minutes.

Frustratingly, though I couldn't seem to get over my own anger and frustration, I was *great* at giving advice to my colleague (typical). One day, to really drive my point home, I exclaimed to him, "Move *on,* motherfucker!"

And in that moment, MOMF (pronounced *momf*) was born.

Every time my colleague and I caught ourselves spiraling into a bad place, we'd MOMF each other. It was amazing how quickly that shifted our mood. It was like a shot in the arm. "Why?" I wondered. "Why does such a tiny thing pack such a punch?"

When I broke it down, I could see why MOMF was magic:

1. Cussing brings emotional relief. That's pretty much what it's for.

2. Calling myself out as a "motherfucker" (in a fun way, not a mean way) let me take responsibility when I was making a bad situation worse.

3. Telling myself to "move on" helped me realize (or remember) that maybe I was clinging to what I *wanted* instead of what was *real.*

4. Finally, for me and my colleague, MOMF was a hilarious secret code, a way to get away with swearing like motherfuckers in our jacked-up, soul-crushing shit show of a workplace.

#*@&*!!

MOMF worked so well for me that I started sharing it with others, including some of the patients in my counseling practice. These were people I had assisted with many of the issues people bring into a therapist's office: troubles with work, love, and family; screwed-up childhoods; illness or chronic pain; outsized feelings of sadness, anger, regret, or shame.

My patients benefited from a lot of the techniques in my therapist repertoire, including gold standards like *mindfulness* and *cognitive behavioral skills* (more about these in a little bit). Interestingly, we found there was often a time and place in their lives when MOMF was the right tool for the job, whether they were struggling to come to terms with a relationship issue or just trying to get through a hard day.

All that work with all those patients with all those different issues convinced me: plenty of us could benefit from adding MOMF to our skill set for getting through life. I've written a lot about MOMF on my blog (https://facebook.com/jeckleberryhunt), and it's insanely fun and rewarding to interact with readers and MOMF users there. This book is my way of teaching you not only the simple concepts of using "move on, motherfucker" in your life but also the evidence-based mindfulness and cognitive behavioral therapy (CBT) skills and techniques that support the MOMF approach. It's a tool kit that can help you not only survive the day but also thrive in life.

SO, WHO'RE YOU CALLING MOTHERFUCKER?

Well, you. (Me too, obviously, but this book is about you.)

I'm calling you a motherfucker—and I haven't even met you. I say it with love. I'm pointing out that you are the one holding yourself back: you are being a motherfucker.

#*@&*!!

How do I know you're getting in your own way? Because you are human, and that is what we do:

We second-guess ourselves.

We have a hard time saying no.

We put others' needs above our own.

We give too many shits about what others think, say, and do.

And when we catch ourselves doing these things, it's time for us to move on, motherfucker. Time to MOMF. I know it's crude, but here's the core of the message:

Calling yourself out can be an act of self-love.

I knew that my work situation was completely messed up and that I needed to accept it for what it was and not take my crappy situation so much to heart. But I *could not get over* my emotions. I wanted to *fix the mess.* I had: the guilt of leaving a good job and choosing a crazy one; the shame of not being able to help others at work who *I felt* wanted me to fix the problems; and the feeling that nothing I did was good enough.

I'll bet that you have felt similar emotions about your life: working in jobs that make you feel crazy, being in relationships wherein you feel guilty or not seen or not good enough, feeling like you have so much around you (and inside you) to fix. I know this because this is the human experience.

When my colleague and I told each other to "move on, mother-fucker," it was more than saying, "Let it go." We already knew with our rational minds that we *should* let go, but we *didn't feel able.* We were using humor and attitude to chip away at the self-defeating emotions of guilt, shame, anger, fear, and powerlessness that we all feel—the emotions that get in the way of finding day-to-day peace. We were acknowledging that we were the ones who needed to handle our problems—and sometimes that means staring down our judging inner voices, laughing at ourselves, and moving on.

MOMF IN A NUTSHELL

When I was a graduate student, I used to meet with my professor for supervision of my counseling work. We had a longstanding, trusting relationship, and I thought he was brilliant. That being said, because I was stubborn and felt I needed to learn things on my own, there were times when I didn't take his advice. I admit that I could be an arrogant asshole.

One day, I was demonstrating my superior wisdom by judging a client's parenting skills. My professor looked at me, smiled, and asked, "Who the hell do you think you are?" He knew this would get my attention, and he was making a point: Who did I think I was to know what was best or even right for the person I was counseling?

Although I bristled in the moment, I've been grateful ever since. If he had tried to explain my mistake to me, I would just have rationalized and told myself that he was the one who didn't understand. Mild as it was, it was the profanity that got my attention. It broke through the professional tone of our meeting to the most important level: our common humanity, including my client's humanity, and her right to respect. It revealed how ridiculous and rigid I was being in judging her. But my professor's smile also let me know that even though he needed to check me, our bond was still strong.

The older I get, the less clear-cut life seems to me. When I was younger, things were black or white, good or bad. Now I see many shades of gray. Just when I think I have the answer, I often realize there

#*@&*!!

are more questions. And when I catch myself becoming all-knowing, I try to say to myself, with a grin, "Who the hell do you think you are?" MOMF uses the same sort of self-talk. It's honest. It's salty but loving, and it cuts the crap.

The MOMF package includes *cognitive behavioral therapy* (CBT) and *mindfulness-based therapy* (MBT) skills, along with good old-fashioned cussing and laughing. Here's a little background on how each of these works for our good. We'll get into the nitty-gritty of these tools in the next chapter.

Cognitive Behavioral Therapy (CBT)

In the 1960s, psychiatrist Aaron Beck described a new therapeutic model, CBT, which teaches how to change our harmful thoughts and actions to healthier ones. CBT gained widespread popularity, particularly starting in the 1990s, because giant piles of evidence showed that it works for many mental health challenges, from depression to obsessive-compulsive disorder to post-traumatic stress.

In CBT, we identify negative, automatic *self-talk*. Self-talk is your own voice in your head that's constantly narrating what's going on and commenting on everything. Though it is you talking to yourself, the tone is sometimes judgmental and negative. Negative self-talk becomes a problem when that voice is unduly harsh or is telling you that everything that you are doing is wrong.

Once we identify self-talk, we methodically change it by using *counter statements* and *thought stopping*—in other words, arguing back with our own unhelpful thoughts. For example, if you discover that you are saying to yourself, "I should try to make others happy," you would **identify** that this thought is not realistic and **argue** back with something like "What evidence do I have that I *can* make others happy, or that it's my job to? Isn't it actually more true that there are no *shoulds* or *have to's?*" Using these techniques consistently over time changes our thought patterns and behaviors, and shifts our feelings too.

Mindfulness

Mindfulness is the state of body and mind being completely present in each moment, and noticing what is happening as it happens, without judging it or ourselves. The concept of mindfulness comes to the West from Buddhist traditions (among others).

Jon Kabat-Zinn[2] popularized a nonreligious, therapeutic version of mindfulness in the United States in the early 1980s. This mindfulness-based therapy emphasizes being aware of what is going on for us from moment to moment: what we are thinking and feeling, what is going on around and within us. It is simply noticing and observing, and continually letting go of judgments or distractions whenever they come up. If you have ever used tools such as a body scan, mindfulness meditation, walking meditation, or the "eating a raisin" exercise, you've encountered some of the basic techniques of mindfulness-based therapy.

Cussing (and Humor)

I recently read that profanity is the new poetry. I agree: when it is used in a skilled or creative way—like poetry—profanity is no longer just a sign of bad manners. It's a powerful mood changer (so is laughter). For it to be effective, the key is to know when and why you are using it.

Cognitive researchers have been studying the use of profanity for years, mostly looking at how other people react when we swear. It is only lately that they've started looking at its emotional benefits. Here's some of what that research has told us so far, a lot of which backs up our everyday experience.

#*@&*!!

- **Cussing increases our tolerance for pain.**[3] When you stub your toe and yell, "Shit!" you are actually helping yourself get through the ouch moment by allowing yourself to feel less pain.

- **More swearing could mean less aggressive behavior.** If we blow off emotional steam with the filthiest words we can come up with, we may be less likely to actually grab someone by the hair or break their windshield.[4-5]

- **Swearing increases social bonding.** It allows us to connect with others and work as a team.[5] A *well-timed* curse can be an icebreaker, cutting through formality and social distance.

- **Cussing is satisfying.** When we learn as children that profanity is forbidden, our brains actually learn to process it differently than ordinary language. Swear words are "special,"[4-5] and this makes them more exciting and fun to use, giving us an emotional release.

- **Used right, profanity provokes laughter.** And laughter protects us against burnout.[6] It reduces physical, emotional, and social tension. It's enjoyable. It's contagious. It leaves us feeling relaxed and ready to laugh some more.

Let's face it, there are times when we all confront terrible circumstances and have no ability to change them—this is the shit show of life. If you can find a way to laugh—even just a little—releasing that emotional tension will give you more head space for rational thought. Profane humor has a special role: it takes the sting out of the painful emotions we feel when life isn't living up to our expectations.

#*@&*!!

You're in Charge

"Move on, motherfucker" is more than just a way to interrupt or stop a distressing thought (CBT), and then replace it with a directive to "let it go" (mindfulness). MOMF takes it for granted that your brain is wired to frequently malfunction. It is wired to be ridiculous. However, MOMF also assumes that you have some choice in what happens next (maybe not *all* the choices or the *best* choices, but some choices). You have the power. You are the motherfucker in charge. Your automatic thoughts don't dictate your destiny—and you don't even have to argue with them. You can just laugh and say to yourself, "Motherfucker is talking again! You know what? Fuck you, crazy ass."

I am deliberately *not* telling you to replace the (unhelpful, automatic) thought with something positive. That works sometimes in some situations, but some situations are just bad, and telling yourself you should see the positive is another form of judging. It does not help. Instead of judgment, I'm saying that you should laugh at yourself. Because you are crazy. I am crazy. We are all crazy. Or, if you prefer, the mind is crazy. Accept it, embrace it, reject it: the choice is yours.

Elizabeth Lesser[7] writes that we are all just "bozos on the bus." We tend to think we're on the bus with those who have crazy lives or crazy families, and that there's another bus for the cool people—those who really have their shit together. But in the end, there is only one kind of bus, and all of us bozos, assholes, motherfuckers, and [insert your own word here] are on it together.

When you call yourself motherfucker, you are acknowledging (with some extra emphasis), "Yep, there I go again, *choosing* to cause problems for myself." There is a lot of benefit to acknowledging and accepting that we are human. We make mistakes. We are clowns at times. Move

#*@&*!!

on, motherfucker hits at the heart of this acceptance and drives home the point of personal responsibility.

Here is how it works. As soon as you notice yourself getting emotionally worked up or becoming overly reactive, take a step back. Reflect on what's going on. Very likely, you will note that you're saying not-super-helpful things to yourself—things like "This shouldn't be happening!" "OMG! I can't believe she just said that!" "Why are you *doing* this to me?" "I can't take this anymore!" And so on.

These kinds of thoughts may be totally justified. But they are dysfunctional *in the situation* because they feed anxiety and feelings of defeat. When you MOMF, you notice these thoughts, label them as dysfunctional, and let them go, saying to yourself, "This shit's jacked. You need to move on, motherfucker."

MAKE MOMF YOUR OWN

When I use the acronym MOMF, I'm talking about a method of using profanity to call yourself out. Which profanity? That's your choice. For me, the word "motherfucker" fits just right. I see it as a synonym for "my friend."

On the other hand, I personally experience "jackass" and "shithead" as insulting. You have to use what works for you. The point is that you are speaking to yourself like a friend—the real, close kind of friend who knows just when and how to call you on your bullshit. You are not being mean-spirited. If you are offended by profanity, if cursing is not at all part of your world, or if you use profanity mainly to abuse others or yourself, then you probably shouldn't use MOMF.

If you use it right, the beauty of the move on, motherfucker phrase—whatever it is for you—is that it's very flexible. You can use it

#*@&*!!

to indicate that you need to MOMF, are in the process of MOMFing (as in "I'm *so* done with this"), or have already moved on ("I've MOMFed that bullshit").

You can also communicate it silently, setting a boundary with your eyes and body language (like sending vibes to stay the fuck away—a protective spell). When I call others motherfucker in my mind, it's with the same intention I have when I say it to myself. I'm speaking to someone who is unaware or doesn't yet know better how to stop something that is hurting them. It's essentially loving, but it means "I am not here for your bullshit."

It can work to use MOMF out loud with people you're close to—you'll be the judge of who and when. Here's a story of when the timing and the person were just right for MOMF. One night, at a get-together on our patio, my husband noticed that our new lawn service had cut down a small boxwood shrub. He railed about it to our guests for a while. I thought he was done, but after the party he started in again: "I'm really upset that they cut down my plant." His internal dialogue was something like "I can't believe it. They must be stupid! I worked so hard growing that plant. They ruined it!"

I looked at him and said, "That is the past. We'll deal with it. Move on, motherfucker."

He looked at me—and then literally (finally) moved on to a new topic.

I've been a psychologist for years. He's accustomed to me doling out advice, and I'm used to him ignoring it. This time, I didn't launch into the research or theory or tell him about a technique he should try. I just hit at the core of the issue with a fact, a promise, a suggestion, and a word that said, "*You're* creating the problem now." It was perfect.

#*@&*!!

WHEN MOMF IS NOT THE RIGHT CHOICE

MOMF is not a cure-all. A lot of folks have had horrible childhoods or other life circumstances that have left them with self-defeating thoughts and behaviors. Some people have suffered great losses, such as the death of a child. Some suffer from severe depression or other mental illness. I would never suggest that these people should or could just "move on."

I don't address the treatment of abuse or grief or psychiatric disorders in this book, because MOMF is not the right tool for these problems. If you are suffering from trauma or a psychiatric disorder, please seek specialized professional care.

At the same time, I am not saying that people who have been abused or have significant grief or depression cannot benefit from MOMFing *relative to daily stress*. They can, with care. It just should not be their *sole* form of therapy but rather another tool in the kit.

I worked with a patient who was abused as a child. We talked in depth about what she had experienced, how it wasn't her fault, and how the experience affects her to this day. She came to an understanding that while she didn't have control as a child, she did have a choice about whether to move beyond the abuse.

Through years of experience in working with survivors of abuse, I have learned that not everyone needs to go back to childhood and dissect everything that happened. For some, it can even be harmful. This young woman preferred to focus on the here and now—and on the past only inasmuch as it affected her present ability to function. Her past isn't forgotten and, of course, it plays a role in the present, but she works to control what role it plays. She doesn't laugh at the past, but she is able to laugh at the present with MOMF.

Again, this approach isn't right for everyone. There are certainly times when a person cannot MOMF because their issues need different

#*@&*!!

kinds of help. But MOMF will always be there when the time is right to use it.

WHEN MOMF IS A GREAT CHOICE

MOMF is perfect for the stress and self-inflicted pain of immediate, present-day situations. It isn't just about telling yourself to keep moving past something. It's about finding your part in a shitty situation. This means noticing what kinds of negative, jacked-up things you are saying to yourself, and how those messages contribute to your jacked-up behaviors. It means accepting the reality of a situation and then making a conscious decision to transcend it. There are times when the "move on" component of move on, motherfucker is literal, and we have to actually leave a situation, but much of the time the movement is *mental and emotional*.

MOMF is ideal for:

- Increasing your self-awareness in tough situations

- Catching and letting go of the negative things you say to yourself habitually

- Changing your patterns of self-defeating behavior

- Managing your daily stress

- Dealing with difficult people and relationships

- Building healthier relationships (and letting go of the unfixable ones)

- Managing disappointment

#*@&*!!

- Managing work stress
- Setting boundaries
- Managing excessive worry
- Overcoming regret
- Managing negative emotions
- Coaching yourself to become a better version of yourself

The situations that drive us crazy are often the ones we cannot control. By going through the MOMF process, we liberate ourselves *even in situations we can't change or master.* We identify what we can't control and focus on what we can—our reactions. We can control our thoughts, feelings, and behaviors by transcending them in our own minds—and sometimes by leaving toxic environments or relationships.

One of my clients who responded well to MOMF as a tool was Peggy, a fifty-year-old executive. She was a real go-getter who prided herself on her integrity, honesty, and work ethic. She believed that her work could have a meaningful impact and wanted to mentor younger leaders. A problem was that she often felt her colleagues were dumping their shit on her. She felt like no one had her back. She wasn't ready to leave her job, but every day felt like another round in the boxing ring, having her ass handed to her.

I suggested that she try move on, motherfucker. She laughed aloud and said the thought of calling her demanding colleagues "motherfuckers" gave her a thrill.

I stopped her to say, "I'm glad you like this idea, but you're the motherfucker."

She asked, incredulously, *"I'm* the motherfucker?"

I said, "Yes, Peggy. You are the motherfucker."

#*@&*!!

She took a moment to reflect, and then I watched the dawning realization that I was telling her she was responsible for her inner state. "Oh, my gosh, *I'm* the motherfucker!"

The point is that once people realize that they are responsible for some part of their pain—maybe a large part—there is relief. We often give up control of our feelings to others. We think others "make us" angry, frustrated, or crazy. Once we realize that we are the motherfuckers in the scenario, we can laugh—and then let go.

Move on, motherfucker is not about self-abuse. You are not calling yourself a name to be mean. Instead, it is meant to get your own attention and to have a crucial conversation with yourself.

Move on, motherfucker is about setting boundaries—with yourself and with others. It's about telling yourself, "Enough already!" You can also use it to communicate an aura of "I'm done with your shit. Move on, motherfucker, and leave me alone." Or you can use it when you need to face up to someone or something. Just the other day, a patient texted me that she imagined herself sending out a vibe of "Bring it on, motherfucker!" She felt herself become unfuckwithable.

Setting boundaries is a way of protecting yourself—holding yourself together, conserving your resources, maintaining sanity, and managing stress. Boundaries promote wellness. It is a way of telling others, "Don't mess with me." We need to admit that we have limited resources and take care how we use them. Once you practice mindfully saying no, it gets easier. This doesn't make you selfish—rather, it's the practice of self-preservation. It allows you to keep giving because you are taking care of yourself too. You quickly realize that you feel better focusing on what you have chosen rather than what you think you have to do. (Tip: If this paragraph has you nodding your head, you'll want to check out chapter 3.)

#*@&*!!

WHAT YOU'LL LEARN IN THIS BOOK

Like I said, move on, motherfucker isn't for everyone or for every situation. It is irreverent. It is crude. It may be shocking to some. But that is why it works so well *in the right situations.*

In this book, you'll learn how the pieces of MOMF (CBT, mindfulness, swearing) fit together to help us out with:

- Cruel self-talk

- A need to control uncontrollable things

- Relationship traps

- Parenting pain

- Work problems

- Health problems

- Bad habits

- Coming to terms with painful past events

- Necessary life changes

In each chapter, you'll read stories about situations I have encountered in my work (these are "composites," or fictionalized accounts based on multiple therapeutic moments). You'll find lots of opportunities to try on what you're reading about, applying it to your own life. At the end of this book, there's a list of recommended reading broken down by topic, plus another list of the references I've used while writing this book.

You'll need a notebook to complete most of the exercises, especially in the next chapter, where you'll pinpoint where your own personal crazy talk is coming from. I also highly recommend that you use a

#*@&*!!

journal to track and record your insights over time. Putting your own words to an experience can help you understand it and file it away for later. Journals can turn into records of just how far you've come—and inspiration for keeping up the good work.

I hope you find something you need here. Let's get started, my motherfuckers!

#*@&*!!

CHAPTER 1

When Your Mind Is a Mess

Fanny couldn't shut off her mind. She worried about bills, friends, her job—a long list of preoccupations. She had a hard time focusing at work. Her fed-up husband told her she needed to stop trying to control everyone and everything. This hurt her feelings—she just needed life to run smoothly. Her dad was also a worrier; he coped by using alcohol. She didn't want this to happen to her.

People like Fanny come to see me, a therapist, because they are in pain. They may call it stress, anxiety, sadness, or low self-esteem, but it all boils down to feeling lousy. The common denominators in most cases are negative self-talk and feelings of defeat. Both are human experiences we all have.

When folks come to me for help, I start by talking with them about how the mind malfunctions in some typical ways. Knowing we're all vulnerable to the same issues just by virtue of being human helps them. (Hell, it saves *my* sanity on a daily basis.) I tell them how our personalities, our beliefs, our self-talk (thoughts and feelings), and our actions work together.

YOU'VE GOT PERSONALITY

We all do. And it might not be what you're thinking it is.

In psychological terms, your *personality* is your general pattern of thoughts, feelings, and desires. It's also part of your mental filter; along with your beliefs, it affects the way you see yourself, other people, and the world in general. Part of your personality comes from nature (genes) and part from nurture (upbringing). You're born with a set of personality traits that come from your parents' genetic contributions. The other half comes from early life experiences.

Take Mo. Mo was bullied mercilessly as a child, and he grew up to be slightly shy and slow to warm up around people. While his shyness likely had some basis in his genes, his early life experiences also played a big role. It's not necessarily important (or actually really possible) to determine which parts of your personality owe more to environment or genes. It's just good to understand how it formed—part genetic, part learned.

Why is this good to know? Because although our personality is pretty stable and set by the time we are adults, the way we use it doesn't have to be. It goes like this:

- Personality can affect beliefs (it also includes beliefs).

- Beliefs affect self-talk (thoughts).

- Self-talk affects our ability to deal with our life, including our behavior (what we choose to do in various situations).

Again, the first item on this list—personality—doesn't really change once you're grown—and there's no reason it should. You are you, you are fantastic and unique, and yes, sometimes and in some situations you are a real motherfucker. We all are.

But you *can* change your beliefs and you can *especially* change your self-talk and your behavior. This means when you are flailing like a motherfucker, you can step back, check yourself, and move on. You can get unstuck and suffer less.

Personality Models

Entire books have been written on personality. I'll make the material simple with a couple of easy-to-relate examples.

The most well-researched model is the *five factor (big five) theory*,[8] a.k.a. OCEAN, which includes five personality traits that we all have to a degree. Here they are:

- **Openness:** being curious and open to new experiences. Openness is related to creativity, inventiveness, and a willingness to try new things and take risks. If you are high on openness, your self-talk might be, "Why not?! Let's see what happens." If you are low, your self-talk might be, "It's scary to try new things. Something might go wrong."

- **Conscientiousness:** doing things with care and vigilance, being self-disciplined, and having follow-through. If you are high on conscientiousness, your self-talk might be, "I can't relax until my work is done right." If you're low, your self-talk might be, "It'll get done eventually. It's not *that* important."

- **Extraversion:** enjoying a high level of social interactions; being warm, engaging, and comfortable in groups. If you're high on extraversion, your self-talk might be, "Being with friends makes me happy." If you're low on extraversion, your self-talk might be, "I prefer being alone."

- **Agreeableness:** needing to get along well with others and cooperate with kindness and consideration. If you are high on

agreeableness, your self-talk might be, "Everyone should like me. I like to keep the peace." If you're low on agreeableness, your self-talk might be, "I don't really care what others want. I'm doing what I want."

- **Neuroticism:** having emotional instability, moodiness, anxiety, and worry; being high maintenance. If you're high on neuroticism, your self-talk might be, "I feel so guilty. I'm just worried about doing the wrong thing. No one really likes me anyway." If you're low on neuroticism, your self-talk might be, "I have a lot of confidence. I trust myself."

Another popular model is based on Carl Jung's typology and was popularized by Katherine Briggs and Isabel Myers.[9] Here are the scales:

- **Introversion vs. extraversion:** where a person gets energy. Introverts get energy from within and prefer to recharge alone. Extroverts get energy from others. They love being around people.

- **Sensing vs. intuition:** how a person prefers to get information. Sensing people prefer to get information from using the five senses. Intuiting people prefer to use their gut.

- **Thinking vs. feeling:** how people make decisions. Thinking people are more logical and rational, more detached, and prefer to make decisions based on rules. Feeling people make decisions based on gut feelings and an overall sense of what is right based on a feeling not derived from rules.

- **Judging vs. perceiving:** how people use information or how they live life. Judging people are organized and planful.

#*@&*!!

Perceiving people are more "go with the flow." They like to keep their options open.

These models are not all-inclusive. There are a lot of other theories out there, all of which give good insight in their own ways; if there's one you like, feel free to use it as you explore your own traits. See the back of this book for some websites for exploring how you fit on the scales above. The purpose of exploring your personality is simply to have a better understanding of how you interact with the world and to better understand the basis for some of your beliefs and self-talk.

What's Your Personality?

Choose a personality trait from one of the models above or one of your own. For example, "I'm introverted" or "I'm a control freak" or "I like to get along with others." Write it down on a blank page in your notebook.

What are some of the beliefs you have that go along with this trait? For example: "Big parties are hard for me, but I like hanging out with a few friends," "I'm shy until I get to know someone really well," or "I need to spend part of the day alone." Write down your beliefs.

Now think of a time when this personality trait has worked really well for you, and write about that. If you can remember it, write down some of your self-talk in that situation that helped you.

Now do the same thing for a situation when this trait did not work out so well for you. What self-talk were you using, and what beliefs were you holding on to in this not-great situation?

If you like, repeat these steps with another personality trait. You can do this now or at any point as you work your way through this book.

This exercise helps you notice that personality traits are never *only* "good" or "bad." Mostly they just are what they are. It's your beliefs about them, and the self-talk you use about them, that can either help you navigate life well or strand you in an ocean of pain.

YOU'VE GOT SOME UNHELPFUL BELIEFS

Beliefs are stable ideas that we see as truths in our own lives. Based on our personalities, we all have *core beliefs* about the world. These core beliefs are based on what we experienced growing up, including what we were taught and what we learned without necessarily being taught, as well as our genetic wiring. These beliefs (which we may not even be aware of) shape every experience we have in the world. Some of them are about ourselves. Core beliefs work like invisible lenses through which all information filters.

For example, George's father left when he was young, and his mom criticized George his whole life, saying he was "just like his dad." "I'm no good" became one of George's core beliefs. Now, when good things happen, he feels unworthy, and when bad things happen, he feels like he is getting what he deserves.

Some of our beliefs cause us a lot of pain. Unlike our personalities, we can change our beliefs if we work at it, though it's not easy. Some common problematic beliefs include:

- "I must always be in control."

- "I am not worthy unless I am doing for others."

- "I am not lovable."

If you tend to see the world around you in a way that reinforces these beliefs, you can bet it's because everything you experience is being run through a limiting belief filter. For example, if you see the world as scary, everything is run through the threatening belief filter. The filter shapes how you view yourself, others, and the world around you in a feedback loop that can be hard but not impossible to break.

What's Your Belief Filter?

Here are some common belief filters. Which, if any, apply to you? You might have more than one. Add your own if these don't quite fit. Some of these can be useful, but taken to an extreme, any of them can also trap you in a view of the world and yourself that blinds you and might even hurt you. What life experiences (positive and negative) do you believe are related to your types of limiting belief filters? Explore these ideas in your journal.

Perfectionist: "Nothing is good enough."

Pessimist: "Things always turn out badly."

Distruster: "People will betray or hurt me."

Pleaser: "I need people to like me or think that I'm a good person."

Self-shamer: "I am completely unworthy and flawed as a person."

Fixer: "It's my job to help others with their problems."

Victim: "Bad things always happen to me."

YOU'VE GOT SOME SHITTY SELF-TALK

Our beliefs directly affect our *self-talk*, which is the voice in our head that's going constantly. It comments on our performance, tells us how great or terrible we are, suggests what we should do, and so on. Negative beliefs make for negative self-talk.

For George, his moment-to-moment self-talk (based on his self-shamer belief filter) is: "I can't get [thing I really want] because I'm not good enough." Or "[Bad thing] is going to happen. Any minute. Just waiting."

#*@&*!!

Negative self-talk causes painful feelings like guilt, sadness, and anxiety. And painful feelings cause self-defeating behaviors like overeating, drinking too much, or becoming a couch potato.

Here are some common negative self-talk statements:

"I'm not good enough."

"I'm not attractive enough."

"I'm not worthy—people will see through me."

"I can't."

"I should _____" or
"I have to _____."

"Bad things always happen to me."

"What if [insert terrible outcome] *happens?"*

There are many more themes and variations on all of these, but you get the idea.

Core beliefs and self-talk can also be positive, of course. If you see things positively, you'll see the upside of situations first. If you see people as basically good, you'll tend to be more trusting.

Positive beliefs lead to positive self-talk, which leads to positive feelings. So if we are feeling happy, it's because we are thinking happy thoughts—saying happy things to ourselves: "Life is awesome." "I can conquer the world." "I love my body and want to show it to others." And so on.

If we're feeling anxious, it's because we're thinking scary thoughts and saying scary things to ourselves: "What if my spouse is cheating on me?" "I wonder if my facial hair will turn into a real beard." "What if my headache is really a brain tumor?" These feelings then shape our behavior, and we do things like read our partner's emails or spend hours googling "lady beards."

When Negative Self-Talk Is Appropriate

When you're paying attention to negative self-talk, you do need to ask yourself if it's justified. There may be times when you think negatively and feel bad because you behaved badly, have unfinished business, or need to do something you are avoiding.

One patient told me that she felt bad because she was a bitch to a friend. When she got done telling me why she felt that way, I nodded. No denying it. She had acted like a bitch and needed to apologize. But it didn't mean that she needed to beat herself up. It just meant that she needed to do something to remedy the situation.

Another patient started a visit by saying that he was up worrying all night. I asked what he was worried about, and he said, "I'm worried that I will lose my house to foreclosure."

I asked, "What makes you think you will lose your house to foreclosure?"

He replied, "I just got a foreclosure notice from the bank."

I thought to myself, "Bud, you better worry!" The worry had a purpose, which was to motivate him to do something to fix a real problem.

Shame, guilt, embarrassment, anger, worry—they have their uses. The idea isn't to get rid of them but to act on them *when they're giving us good information*—and to kick them to the curb when they are not.

#*@&*!!

YOU'VE GOT SOME CHOICES

Personality, beliefs, thoughts, self-talk, feelings: they're all in the mix. Some you can change, some you can't. You know what you have the best shot at changing?

What you do. Your behaviors. Your choices.

Let me tell you about the Buddhist concept of the *second arrow*. It goes like this: If you are struck with an arrow, it hurts like hell. You can't change that the arrow struck you. That part is done. Getting to safety and getting help are your jobs now. When you bitch and moan about the tragedy of the arrow striking you, you create your own suffering—in addition to your original wound. In other words, you are shooting yourself with a second arrow.

This second arrow concept is so crucial to MOMF that I include second arrow stories throughout this book. These stories emphasize that although bad things happen in life that we can't control, we *can* control how we handle them. We can control whether we make it worse. We are not accountable for our wound, but we are accountable for our responses—including moving on from the wound.

To be clear, there are circumstances when "move on" is not the humane response, such as our grief over the loss of a child. Some responses are near inevitable based on our individual histories and just our human nature. We may crawl into bed and pull the covers up. We may cry to our friends. We may think about giving up. We all have these responses. And they're all normal responses to the first arrow. Mindfulness, CBT, and other healing methods can still help us if "living with" rather than "moving on" is what's called for.

The problem is when we get stuck there, when we don't eventually pick ourselves up and move on. When we feel *unable* to recover. Worse yet is when we tell ourselves, "This shit *shouldn't* be happening." Because it *is* happening. I'm talking about the negative events of everyday life

#*@&*!!

that are worsened when we hang on to the feeling of being a victim past a certain point.

And the degree to which it will stop hurting us? That's mostly up to us.

Take Fanny. In *personality* terms, Fanny is a worrier (she's neurotic, according to the OCEAN model). She is also very conscientious (her dad was also a big worrier, but maybe less conscientious). Her *beliefs* include, "I have to pay attention to the important things or they'll go wrong—and it will be my fault" and "Avoiding my responsibilities is not okay."

Fanny's *self-talk*—the tape that's playing constantly in her head—goes something like this while she's at home having dinner with her husband: "Was the equation in that one spreadsheet cell wrong? It might be wrong. What if it was wrong? That would mean I'm a sloppy idiot and I could be taken off the team. I've got to check it. Should I call my supervisor at home? How am I going to get any sleep if I don't? But what will she think if she learns about my mistake? Ugh, that was so stupid!" And on and on. She's not really at dinner with her husband. He notices, and it's not a great scene.

Fanny's a good worker and she loves her husband and her friends. She's someone you can depend on. But in this moment, she's also kind of a motherfucker. She has picked up that second arrow and is stabbing herself for all she's worth. She might feel like she can't help it, but she can. Motherfucker can learn to move on.

What Are Your Core Beliefs?

What are some of your core beliefs? In your notebook, write down two or three beliefs you hold about the world and your place in it. For example, "It's my job to get things done" or "Men are dogs."

What negative self-talk do you have to go with those beliefs? For example, "I can't ask for help" or "I won't ever have a good relationship."

What important life experiences do you believe shaped those beliefs and that self-talk? Write about any you can think of, and feel free to come back to add more later.

Finally, what parts of your personality do you think add power to those core beliefs? For example, if you are very empathetic and you were a caretaker for a dysfunctional parent as a child, you may believe that it's your job to help other people who are suffering. That belief may lead you to behaviors that burn you out. Write down your thoughts.

MOMF Tools in Action

Fanny shows us how the whole personality → belief → self-talk chain looks in action—one ruined dinner at a time. In this section, we'll watch Randy, Sid, and Niari work through their shit with their own personal versions of MOMF. Randy goes heavy on CBT techniques, mindfulness is Sid's go-to, and Niari does it all. She figures out how to put down the second arrow and Move. The fuck. On. Then she works in the longer-term, slow-burn techniques of CBT and mindfulness too. Pieces of their stories are interwoven with the tools and practices they've learned to use—and that you can learn to use too.

USING CBT TOOLS

The "cognitive" in "cognitive behavioral therapy" refers to what you are thinking. And so one aspect of CBT involves identifying your negative self-talk. It's the easiest place to start, because self-talk is always there, commenting on everything you think and do. You can then counter negative self-talk as it happens ("No, I am not evil incarnate. In fact, I'm pretty nice."). You can also work backward from the self-talk

#*@&*!!

and identify your core beliefs. Then you can look at those to see if they're beliefs you want to keep or try to change.

The "behavioral" aspect of CBT refers to what you do. Changing your behaviors, when needed, is part of the therapy too. There are times when you just can't shut off the nastiness in your head. In those situations, you often can still change your behavior. You can get up and move to a different room. You can exercise instead of emotional eating. Choose to do something other than going over the negative thoughts again and again. You may find that your stressful thoughts go away because you are distracting yourself.

Bottom line: CBT means methodically identifying your thought patterns and where they come from, understanding how they affect your feelings and behaviors, changing those thought patterns, and changing your behaviors. The intended result is improved feelings.

Randy's Story

Randy's dad drank a lot when Randy was growing up, and he used to call Randy names likes "lazy" and "loser." Randy grew up to be a self-shamer. Now he struggles to feel worthy of anything. His negative self-talk is, "You'll never amount to anything. Your own dad didn't even love you."

In therapy, Randy gave some thought to his early life experiences and to the traits and beliefs that ran in his family. Using CBT, Randy was able to develop two important skills: identify negative beliefs about himself, the world, and other people; and identify how those beliefs negatively affect his self-talk, how his negative self-talk makes him feel, and the problems it causes in his life.

After a lot of broken relationships, Randy has made some connections between his past and his present. He appreciates

#*@&*!!

understanding the connections and how they contribute to his actions, but he's not out of the woods. For instance, he feels like he finally found love with Lila, but he keeps thinking that she'll cheat on him. He behaves in ways that show he doesn't trust her. This has caused a lot of fights. He notices that his core beliefs, self-talk, and behaviors are putting his relationship in jeopardy, and he needs this to stop.

Randy uses the skill of questioning his thoughts. He asks, "What is the evidence that what I'm saying to myself is true?" In other words, he has to prove that his statement is true or admit that he's simply torturing himself. If there is actual evidence, he must ask himself what he needs to do about it. If there is no evidence, he has to accept that he's making problems that don't exist.

For instance, Randy thinks, "Lila is so friendly to other people." Fair enough; Lila's great. But then he goes straight to "I can tell that she wants to cheat on me, because deep down she knows that I'm a loser." Yet, Randy has no evidence that Lila is cheating on him, that she wants to cheat on him, or that she thinks he's a loser. He only has his negative thoughts and feelings—his fear about what might happen.

So Randy uses counterstatements to argue back with the negative things he says to himself. A counterstatement can be thought of as what a good friend might say, or another way to look at the situation.

To separate what's true in the present from what his past taught him to fear, Randy developed this counterstatement: "Lila is a friendly person, which is why I like her so much. It doesn't mean that she wants to be with someone else. She is with me, after all, and no one is forcing her."

#*@&*!!

Randy also uses behavioral strategies (actions, that is) to interrupt his negative thoughts. When he starts to think of Lila cheating, he purposely gets his mind on something else by calling a friend and talking about another subject, going outside, exercising, or reading a book.

He also uses positive affirmations or coaching statements to counter the negative self-talk, give himself focus, and improve his mood. Randy chooses to say to himself: "I am strong enough to resist my habits," "I am worthy and deserve to be happy," and "I choose to let go of the past."

When those lying old thoughts come up, Randy has to make a stand and fight them back before he can move on from them. It was hard work in the beginning, but it's getting easier the more he does it. He's shared with Lila what he's doing and why, and she's on his side.

USING MINDFULNESS TOOLS

So what is mindfulness, aside from a word that apparently needs to be on 88 percent of all magazine covers? All it means is: becoming more aware of what is going on, what you are thinking, and how you are feeling—all without judging or critiquing. Call it noticing.

You will often hear the term "mindfulness" associated with meditation, but meditation is just a very effective tool to improve mindfulness. You can also develop it by making a habit of asking yourself to observe the present moment through your five senses. However you practice it, mindfulness teaches you to stop reacting to what is going on around you. Instead, you just try to notice it and return to your body, your breath, the room, the moment. You are still observing events (traffic

#*@&*!!

noise, a bird singing) and how you feel (hungry, achy). But you are learning that you don't immediately need to *do* anything about what you observe. Slowly, you become able to develop a thoughtful response to whatever comes up.

Mindfulness doesn't target the *content* of your thoughts or whether those thoughts are valid. It's just practicing becoming present in each moment while it is happening without judgment. The idea is to learn from what is happening in the present moment through *reflection* rather than *rumination*.

Rumination is when you keep thinking the same negative thoughts over and over, causing yourself distress. For example, you might say to yourself, "I finished the work assignment, but it was crappy. I should have done a better job. I'm probably going to be fired. My boss probably thinks I'm an idiot. I wish I had asked for help from my coworker, but she thinks I'm lazy. No matter what I do, I'm screwed. This always happens to me." And so on. Rumination is like pouring gas on a fire.

Reflection, on the other hand, is noticing and studying your thoughts and reactions without buying in to or judging them. For example, you might reflect by saying, "I completed the work assignment but it was crappy. Oh, there are my 'not good enough' thoughts again. Wow. Those come up a lot." Reflection lets the fire die by not giving it more fuel.

How does this look in practice? Let's take the example of pain, which is a necessary part of life. Imagine you have a side cramp: it is very uncomfortable but not serious. You can ruminate about how awful it is and about all the things it's keeping you from doing. Or you can notice that there isn't anything you can do except wait for the pain to pass. And it does pass. That is the same thing as sitting with any emotional discomfort. Eventually, it passes because life is ever-changing.

#*@&*!!

Sid's Story

Sid feels chronically unhappy with his life but isn't sure why. He just knows he's unfulfilled and he's afraid his life has no meaning. He decides to use mindfulness tools and principles to better understand his situation and move toward a meaningful life. He begins to become aware of how he is feeling while he is feeling it, to become aware of how he is thinking while he is thinking it, and to practice paying attention to events as they happen.

Sid begins to start each day with a series of deep breaths. While breathing deeply, he purposefully notices how his body feels. Also at least once a day, Sid forces himself to go for a quick walk down the hall and notice how his body feels. If he gets a chance to go outside, he makes a point of looking up and noticing the sky and how the air smells.

He also starts journaling at the end of the day, just noticing all that happened in his day, including what he thought and how he felt about it. Sid also asks himself what he appreciated most about his day, and he writes that down. One recurrent message he notices is, "Don't judge your thoughts or feelings. Just notice them."

Sid begins to notice other patterns in his journaling and in his thought processes. He finds that he is prone to feeling like a victim, and he tends to focus on how powerless he feels. He practices viewing these thought patterns as a tendency he happens to have, while not getting caught up in blaming himself for having them.

Sid identifies that when he focuses on how helpless he feels, he is making the situation worse. (Remember the second arrow? This is it.) Over time, he develops a better understanding of his tendencies and a better ability to accept them so that he can work to let

#*@&*!!

them go. He begins to understand that letting go doesn't mean getting rid of his negative self-talk—just not getting caught up in it.

As Sid learns to listen to how he is feeling while he is feeling it, it becomes easier for him to identify what emotional baggage is being triggered. This new awareness allows him to just notice what is happening and not respond. He learns to say to himself, "Let it go," "Let it be," "Things are as they are," "It is what it is," and "It is just the way it is supposed to be."

Sid also learns another important mindfulness skill: focus his purposeful attention on what he is doing for a few minutes each day and just be. Sid stops looking at his smartphone, computer, television, books, magazines, and mail while he eats his meals. He tries to appreciate how food tastes while he chews and takes his time while eating. He then decides to start doing one thing at a time and stop multitasking. He sets other technology-free times.

To his surprise, he finds that his life is a lot more satisfying than he had thought. He didn't have to make big changes to his circumstances—no new job, new town, new relationship, or new house. He just had to pay more attention to what was already there!

Mindfulness can be practiced in nearly every situation. It is particularly helpful when you are feeling uncomfortable. When you notice painful feelings or thoughts, ask yourself if the pain is telling you something useful or pointing to something you need to make right. If the painful feeling is self-created, then maybe you could choose to let go of some aspect of the situation. To do this, first sit with the uncomfortable feeling. Let it be. Notice your mind judging, and call it what it is.

Sometimes situations bring up baggage from the past. Be sure to tell yourself that you don't have to open the baggage. Remember that just because you have a negative feeling doesn't mean that you have done

#*@&*!!

something wrong. Perhaps the play button got pushed on the story of trying to please, trying to fix, or feeling unworthy. Stay in the present moment. As your mind wanders back to the past, return it to the present, over and over. That is mindfulness—the practice of returning to the moment at hand without judgment.

USING FOUL-LANGUAGE TOOLS

As you learned in chapter 1, move on, motherfucker is an approach to living that combines CBT, mindfulness, and holding yourself accountable with salty language (bonus: while laughing your ass off whenever possible). Let's look at how cussing—and other MOMF tools—worked for one client.

Niari's Story

When Niari doesn't get the promotion she wanted, she is devastated. She calls in sick for two days and isolates herself from friends and family for more than a week. Even after she drags herself back to work in fear of losing the job that she is now sure she hates (though she liked it well enough before losing the promotion), she still can't bring herself to talk to anyone. Avoiding texts, calls, and social media starts to feel weird, then bad, then like its own problem.

That's when Niari takes action. She realizes that she is stabbing herself with the second arrow and identifies how she is making a bad situation worse. So she calls herself out for the role she is playing in the scenario.

When caller ID shows her sister calling for the third time, she says to herself, "Motherfucker, please," takes a deep breath, and picks up. Some of that conversation is a little awkward ("Sorry I didn't pick up or call back, and that you were worried...") but mostly

#*@&*!!

it feels good. She gets to vent and cry to someone who cares about her, and she is able to return other texts and calls, and post a non-crazy update or two on social media. Second arrow neutralized.

Niari learns an important MOMF lesson: remind yourself that you have choices. Niari can't control when bad things happen, but she can choose what she does in response. She can choose to stab herself with the second arrow, or she can move on with her life.

Niari acknowledges to herself that if she doesn't stop acting and thinking like a wounded animal at work, she'll be facing another second-arrow scenario. She didn't get the promotion, but she still has a job, and she can still make plans for her career. Being cold, bitchy, and unreliable at work can put both her job and her career in jeopardy. She needs to be a professional and focus on getting her head right about what happened, what it means (which might be different from what she thought it meant), and what she can do in the future. It is time to look at the long game, learn what she can from the situation, and have a bunch of non-shitty days in the process.

Niari often catches herself feeling like a victim, saying to herself that she has been shafted at work, and that no matter what she does, she will always be screwed over. She spends some time journaling about this self-talk. Her core belief is that "People will take advantage of you if they can," and some of the life stories that fed her core belief include that both her parents relied on her to take on more responsibility than she was ready for as a child and then claimed her successes as their own.

Niari forces herself to prove the self-talk and her core belief with evidence from her own life, and she can't. In fact, she admits to herself that her coworker who got the promotion had worked her ass off and deserved the advancement. She also remembers a few times when she had, in fact, come out on top in an important competition. Niari is not always the loser in life. It's when she loses out on something that matters so much to her idea of herself that she feels like she is truly a loser.

When sadness comes up, Niari uses mindfulness. She allows herself to sit with her sadness and notice the hurt. She practices letting it come and go, and notices when she tries to hold on to it. This is not the time for sass or a pep talk, but for letting her real feelings have their moment.

To help snap herself out of her depressed moods, Niari thinks of what her friend Tina would say: "Oh, bitch, please…. We don't have time for this shit." She imagines a soap opera narrator saying: "On today's episode of The Festive and the Fucked, shit happens." She conjures what her queenly aunt would say: "Shit show doesn't look good on you, my dear." And finally, Niari figures out what would get her off her ass with a laugh: "Déjà Moo, princess. This bullshit smells familiar. Peace out, girlfriend!"

Think about what salty language would give you a good laugh and a kick in the ass when you need it. Call yourself out when you are making yourself feel worse. Argue back with yourself. Let a situation slide off you. And motivate yourself to do the next right thing.

Finally, pick some CBT tools and mindfulness practices that you think might work for you to feel better on a daily basis and be your best self going forward.

Is MOMF for You?

I'm guessing that this isn't the first self-help book you've read, but it might be the first one that prescribes profanity. When you think about the MOMF method, what is appealing compared to other things you've tried? What ele-

#*@&*!!

ments sound like a good fit for you at this point? What lights your fire? Why are you reading this book? What do you really want to change? Write down your answers in your journal.

I hope the next eight chapters will help you find where MOMF can make your life better, whether the battleground is work, parenting, relationships, illness, bad habits, jacked-up life circumstances, or your own messed-up mind. We're all motherfuckers making our way in this world. When you use MOMF, you're not putting yourself down, you're setting yourself right. So do it with love, power, and the kind of laughter that gets your ass moving.

MOMF Like a Mofo

- **Start to journal daily.** Some people get caught up in the "rules" for journaling. There are no rules other than to do it regularly so that it becomes more routine. Just get in the groove of writing about your day, your thoughts, and your feelings. Note your patterns of negative thinking and see if you can identify the negative beliefs that underlie the thoughts. Start to argue back, using your own style of profanity. In later chapters, you'll get more specific journaling direction; for now, just free flow.

- **Start exercising every day.** Do it for a total of fifteen to thirty minutes, even if you break it up at morning, noon, and night. The point is to get yourself moving physically and mentally.

#*@&*!!

CHAPTER 2

When You Need to
Stick Up for Yourself

Meet Shep.

Shep is a single parent who feels like a doormat at work and at home. Coworkers dump extra work on him last minute and take credit when projects are completed. He sometimes ends up working at least ten extra (unpaid) hours in a week. He *can't* say no: he wants to be a team player.

When Shep gets home, he cooks, cleans, shops, runs his kids to and fro. It's up to him to make it all run smoothly. When he tells his kids to help out, they ignore him. He *can't* push them: they might go live with their mom.

Shep's parents give him a weekly list of things they need done at their house that they can't do on their own. He *can't* say no: they're old.

When Shep came to me for help, we talked some about why he's an emotional hostage and user-magnet in every part of his life. Basically, he's a fixer whose self-talk is on the theme "I have to help or bad things will happen." Shep needs to ignore his feelings of paralysis and just practice enunciating the word "Nnnnoooo!"

No to his parents' demands. But he can help them develop a new plan.

No to being the sole cook, maid, and chauffeur. Stop giving the kids privileges until they help out.

And hell no to coworkers who expect him to do their jobs. No need for a plan or explanation, just "Hell no."

But if you're like Shep, how do you get from "Yes, sir, absolutely" to "Nope"? One way is in understanding—and shifting—your communication style.

COMMUNICATION STYLES

Let's say you are at a nice restaurant with friends. The food is expensive. You've been looking forward to it, and everyone is having a good time. Your rocky mountain oysters arrive, and they're…actually kind of nasty. Do you:

A) Become enraged, call the waiter over, and start yelling, "Hey, shithead, I'm paying a lot of money for this crap. WTF?!"

B) Think, "Oh well, the food sucks, but I don't want to cause a scene. I'll just order something different next time."

C) Quietly call the waiter over, explain the dish isn't what you'd hoped, and request that he take it back. Ask if you can order something else.

If you chose answer B, you're like a lot of people. (Also, this chapter is for you.)

People who "eat it anyway" don't want to make others feel uncomfortable. They make other people's comfort (real or imagined) more important than their own best interest or desires. They rationalize this. They tell themselves (and sometimes others) that the food wasn't *that* bad—they just wouldn't order it again. They'll deal with it this time. No biggie. Except it isn't just this time, it's every time.

Let's take a tour of communication styles. There are three.

Answer A is an **aggressive response**. It's saying that your needs are more important than anyone else's. The self-talk here is, "I can't believe I'm being treated this way. These people are idiots!" When you're aggressive, forcefully standing up for yourself, you are also stepping on the rights and feelings of others. Aggressive people often have insecurity at their core, which they deal with by making sure they are treated with respect, goddamn it! They might have a perfectionist or distrusting belief filter. All things considered, they might get their way in the moment but face a lot of backlash down the line (which is often totally fine by them).

Answer B is a **passive response**. Underlying the passive response is a belief that others' needs are more important than yours. Depending on your belief filter and style, your self-talk might be, "What will others think of me if I complain?" (pleaser) or "This is my fault. I'm such an idiot. I should have known better than to order that" (self-shamer) or "This always happens to me. I get the shit end of the stick" (victim).

Answer C is an **assertive response**. It shows that you recognize that while you're not the only patron in the restaurant, you're paying a lot of money to dine there. You want to enjoy your food. The self-talk is, "Wow, it's a little awkward, but I really don't want to eat this. I deserve to enjoy the food I paid for. I'll ask if I can get something else. Let's see what my options are." Assertive communicators recognize that their needs are as important as everyone else's—not necessarily more important, but definitely not less. Assertive communicators act in a way that conveys their own needs and wants, but are respectful to all parties and open to a solution that's acceptable to the kitchen and waitstaff as well as themselves.

#*@&*!!

What's Your Style?

What kind of communicator are you? (If you're not sure, consider what your friends, family, or coworkers would say about your communication style.)

Do you have different styles depending on where you are (home, work, family visit) or with whom you're communicating (spouse, child, parent, client)?

Think of a couple of specific examples of you using your most common communication style. How well does that style generally work for you? If you can, think of an example or two of when you used a different style. What was that like?

Would you like to be able to use a different style? What are your biggest fears around this? (Hint: Those fears can clue you in to your belief filters, if you haven't identified them already.)

Being assertive (rather than passive, aggressive, or the worst of both worlds, passive-aggressive) means you don't have to choose between being a doormat and being an asshole. You can still have your same personality and a lot of your same beliefs about yourself as a good or kind or helpful person. You can even still have your same crazy-ass self-talk going on behind your eyeballs. The difference is in what comes out of your mouth. Change that, and you've got your best chance at changing the rest.

The bottom line is to take a risk and make a move—to find that MOMF moment and lean in to it. I promise that if you do, the world won't fall apart.

Once you act differently, it becomes easier to act differently again. And once you get used to choosing different actions, you can step back and get a clearer picture of what's going on inside your head and within the situation. With some experience, you'll start to see that what you did (just say nope) was the right choice—even if it doesn't feel familiar. The more you do it, the better you'll feel.

#*@&*!!

People around you may not like that you're saying no, because they have to do whatever it is you declined to do for themselves—and that's probably always been the sticking point, hasn't it? But they'll learn. Or they'll walk away, which may end up being a relief anyway. There will be pain associated with change, but just notice it with mindfulness and see where it leads. The pain doesn't mean that you have done something wrong that needs to be fixed. It just means that you're growing.

There's little doubt that people trapped in a passive communication style get the short end of a lot of sticks. They tend to have belief filters that are not fun at all: victim, self-shamer. They may also have belief filters that work super well sometimes (fixer), but they get trapped in cycles whereby their superpower becomes their superweakness.

FEEL THE FEAR AND DO IT ANYWAY

It's a fact: assertiveness—actually, lack of assertiveness—is at the core of a lot of my work with patients. When people come to see me saying they feel terrible about themselves, it often becomes clear that it's because they don't protect themselves. It's no wonder they feel lousy. Tolerating others' monkey business conveys the message that it's okay with you to be treated poorly.

Maya's Story

Maya came to me saying, "I have low self-esteem. I want to work on feeling better about myself." As we talked, I learned she was in a relationship with someone who had cheated on her several times. When he explained why he cheated, it somehow came down to being Maya's fault. She took him back each time, telling herself that she would try harder.

#*@&*!!

Maya was a self-shamer who could never win in her own eyes. She criticized herself for not being good enough to keep her boyfriend faithful, and she criticized herself for staying with someone who treated her this way.

Maya also felt stuck and unappreciated at work. She was a computer programmer, a field dominated by men, and she never seemed to get promoted as they did. She had a good education and worked her ass off. Intellectually, she knew she deserved better, but emotionally she was reluctant to demand more—because she wasn't sure that she was good enough to get more.

Maya has a lot of company: people who don't stand up for themselves because they feel fear—fear of being left by a partner or losing a job or alienating a friend. They fear that all of the terrible things they are saying to themselves might actually be true. I understand those fears, but let me tell you: whenever the fear is in charge, you've lost control of your life. Your inner motherfucker is driving the bus; don't be surprised when you end up in crazy town.

Playing it too safe can make you feel like you're dying a slow death inside. You could just as easily discover that you feel relief to be away from a partner who cheats on you, or a job where you aren't appreciated, or a friend who is never there for you. Likewise, fear of failing can keep you from even trying to build relationships or a career that feeds you. Slow death. No good.

Being assertive means demonstrating to yourself and others that you are worth the fight. If you aren't willing to stand up and protect your own rights, your own boundaries, your own emotions, it's unlikely others will.

Assertiveness is not about being a jerk, and it isn't selfish. It is about communicating to others that you are a person with value, worth defending. When people worry too much about what others will think, I say, "So, you'd rather leave yourself up shit creek so that others will think you're nice? Do you really want to care if someone approves of you taking care of yourself? Does it really matter if people think you're nice if, in the end, you're left feeling screwed over?" I can't see a path to higher self-esteem and self-confidence without a willingness to stand up for oneself when necessary. And it's something that can be learned.

SPEAK YOUR TRUTH, THEN STFU

Psychologists have identified some techniques for keeping your calm while you keep your boundaries. One of the best is "I" statements.

"I" statements let you tell your truth without making it about someone else. For example, "I feel like you don't respect me when you make an agreement and then don't keep it." The foundation of this technique is the use of the word "I." You take responsibility for your feelings and stand up for yourself:

- "I can't do that project for you."

- "I feel cheated when you take all the credit."

- "I feel that I'm being passed over for promotions, despite all the extra work I've done this year."

If you're used to being a passive communicator, you've probably spotted a problem with those "I" statements. By saying what you think, feel, and need—and then shutting your mouth—it feels like you're losing control of the situation. You're possibly causing a bad feeling in the other person. You're not making it better for the other person in advance. You're not identifying the problem *and* fixing it with the same statement. *Bad things might happen!*

#*@&*!!

But here's the MOMF moment:

You speak your truth.

Then you shut your mouth.

It's the other person's turn now.

You need to get to the place where you can accept that if the other party doesn't receive the message well, they now have something to think about.

Practice Being Assertive

Start by noticing when you feel the drive to please others. Then make a choice:

- **Develop some MOMF counterstatements.** Talk back to your negative self-talk. You might say, "There I go again, trying to make everyone happy. Fuck that. I'm so done with that." Or "No way, motherfucker! Not going there today."

- **Redirect.** Jot down some things you can do to get your mind off of guilt and shame, such as call a good friend or leave the room and go for a walk.

- **Be mindful of painful feelings.** Try to spend five minutes noticing and accepting your feelings by breathing through them.

- **Use affirmations.** And make your "I" statements extra salty: "I am a strong motherfucker." And "Fuck this! I deserve to be happy." Think of your own MOMF "I" statements and write them down in your journal.

Putting yourself out there is excruciating. But rest assured: a *necessary* confrontation isn't good or bad. It just is. The challenge is to not get so caught up in anxious self-talk that you somehow feel you "caused" the other person to feel bad or that you won't be liked or that you did something wrong. Fuck that. This isn't about *you*. It's about you being honest about bullshit and communicating that people can take it elsewhere.

Easy for me to say, right? But you can do it.

The anxiety you feel following difficult conversations is *just a feeling* associated with doing something different. Standing up for yourself goes against dysfunctional core beliefs or emotional garbage that says everyone should like us or be happy with us. A counterstatement to that is, "What kind of life do you have if you are living it for someone else's pleasure?"

After a difficult conversation, you need to stop and acknowledge that you said what needed to be said. You were honest. The other person may not have been ready to hear it, but that's the other person's baggage, not yours. You can't "make" someone angry, sad, happy, or any other emotion. It's not your responsibility, and it's not within your power.

If your loving heart shrinks from the idea of not protecting others' feelings, consider this: when you try to take responsibility for others' emotions, you don't allow them to grow. Whether something was the right thing to say or do is not directly related to how someone takes it. (Of course, I'm not talking here about when you deliberately say hurtful things to another person; then *you* may be the one who deserves to be confronted. I mean, you do have to have some tact.) Sometimes people misunderstand your intention, but if you behaved in an appropriate way, your job is not to "fix" someone else's pain.

Don't hold back from the confrontation. Embrace it! Confrontation gets a bad rap. People think of it negatively, but I see confrontation as simply addressing something that's just too important to gloss over. Take your time and give thought and care to how you approach

#*@&*!!

it—you're building new skills and it takes work. But do address it head-on so that you can move on with your life. The buildup to confrontation—the fantasizing and distortion—tends to be much worse than the actual outcome. That is why the sooner you're done with it, the better you will feel. That is not to say that you always get what you want in the end, but you win one every time you treat yourself with respect.

Beating Yourself Up

Think about the last time you had a difficult conversation with someone. What things did you say to yourself that created self-pain and torture (the second arrow)? Where does this self-flagellating tendency come from? After you beat yourself up, how did that affect your feelings, behavior, and what happened next?

PAIN HURTS FOR A REASON

When I was in graduate school, I came to deeply understand that pain can be the best way to instigate deep, meaningful change. There were times when I said things to people I meant to help that I wish I could take back. There were times, out of ignorance mostly, when I acted like a know-it-all and said things that may have hurt more than helped. There were absolutely times when I tried so hard to help people fix their problems that I got in the way of their healing. These mistakes were painful, but there was so much to learn. If I didn't feel the pain, I couldn't learn the lesson.

Reflecting on why you have pain or what your role is in a situation or what needs to change can be a critical moment in your personal growth process. To get in the way of that for another person is wrong.

#*@&*!!

Following the death of George H. W. Bush, I heard that he said to his granddaughter that he loved her too much to stop her from making her own mistakes. It is a hard thing to do, but it is the better thing to do.

My point is that after you have had a critical conversation, you need to step back and be mindful of how you feel. Note any negative emotions, what triggered them, and what core beliefs from your past baggage are affecting your present—and then decide what to do about it.

Next, tell yourself to move right along, motherfucker. Your challenge is not to get caught up in the emotional quicksand, where you begin to drown in negative self-talk that says, "I'm such a terrible person." Ask yourself how well you conveyed what needed to be said.

How to Communicate Assertively

You'll need to practice being assertive using some of your CBT and mindfulness skills. Here's the breakdown:

1. Identify a situation where you're avoiding conflict.

2. Consider which aspects of your personality, your story, your core beliefs, and your self-talk are leading you to avoid the conflict.

3. Write down your self-talk statements ("He'll be mad"), and for each of them try to find evidence ("I've never tried it, so I actually don't know he'll be mad").

4. Now find the evidence on the other side ("If I don't say anything, I'll feel shitty the rest of the day") and make some counterstatements ("He might get mad. But I'll feel better. It's worth a try and I'll see what happens.").

5. After the conversation, give yourself some time to process what happened.

The more you practice at being assertive, the better you'll get. The more you stand up for yourself, the less likely it is someone will dump shit on you at work or at home. You won't be seen by others as weak, and you will see *yourself* as someone who's strong. The internal dialogue that tells you that you *have to* do things for others or you *have to* keep the peace or you *have to* take shit from others will fade. You'll learn that the more you give in to your negative self-talk, the more you are enabling others around you to act in selfish ways.

MOMF Like a Mofo

- **Journal about your efforts to change your communication style.** Notice how you feel and how things unfold. Monitor your practice of communication changes over time. How are you doing? What adjustments need to be made?

- **Practice saying no.** Ask yourself, "What went well? What didn't feel quite right? What do I need to let go of?" Write about this.

#*@&*!!

CHAPTER 3

When You're a Control Freak

Tab grew up with parents who drank—a lot. Now Tab's an adult with a family of her own. Her parents still drink a lot, and they're a handful. And she still feels obligated to take care of them. Her sister also drinks heavily, and her brother never wants to talk about any problems.

On holidays, Tab has everyone over to her house for dinner, and she spends weeks preparing and worrying about how things will unfold.

Her self-talk is, "What if my parents cause a scene? What if my sister gets drunk? What can I do to make sure everyone has a nice time and things go smoothly?" She clings to the belief that if she plans well enough and functions highly enough, she can engineer the kind of holiday get-together that families have on Pinterest.

Care to guess how well that tends to work out for her?

CONTROL IS AN ILLUSION

I meet a lot of people like Tab in my therapy practice: folks who respond to crazy scenarios in their lives by trying to control them, folks who choose to have a relationship with craziness and who keep getting exasperated, or mad, or heartbroken when craziness shows up.

And I get why they do it: mostly they grew up in families where they learned it was their job to be the sane person in a crazy house. They swallowed the message that if they do everything right, things will work out well. The problem being that controlling our lives isn't possible for anyone. Like, not one single one of us is within three light-years of it. But man, do they keep trying. They end up acting like total assholes, or feeling like shit, or both. Beneath the surface is a mess of shame, guilt, anger, and fear.

Long story short: too many of us are stuck in a control trap. MOMF can help.

A need to control, like any personality-tinged belief pattern, is part genetic and part learned. If you're reading this chapter, perhaps you think control or perfectionism is a problem for you (if you think it's a problem for someone else in your life, you need to go to chapter 4 for some real talk about codependence). You can investigate your relationship with control by doing the next exercise, which will give you focus for the rest of the chapter.

Your Inner Control Freak

What are some of your core beliefs about being perfect, being good, or being in control? In your journal, write down as many as you can think of. What are your strongest two or three beliefs about being in control?

What negative self-talk do you have that goes with these beliefs? Write down any self-talk that springs to mind (you can add to this list later if more pop into your head).

What important life experiences do you believe shaped these beliefs and your self-talk? Write about any you can think of, and feel free to come back to add more stories or more details later.

What parts of your personality do you think add power to these core beliefs?

JUST LET THE BANANA GO

Jon Kabat-Zinn[2] talks about how monkeys are caught in India. People wire a coconut to a tree with a hole cut in the front that will allow a

#*@&*!!

monkey to put its hand in but not pull its fist out. A banana is hidden inside the coconut. The monkey puts its hand inside the coconut and grabs the banana. At that point, the monkey cannot pull its hand out unless it lets go of the banana. The monkey generally doesn't let go.

Trying to control is like hanging on to the banana. As long as we cling to the banana, we are trapped. As soon as we let go and say, "Fuck it. It is what it is rather than what I want it to be," we are free. When you try too hard to control, you end up with no control. In fact, the drive to control controls you. Be smarter than the monkey.

What Bananas Do You Need to Let Go Of?

In what areas of your life is your drive to control not working for you anymore? This could be work, family, health, a relationship, or a situation. Jot down (or write paragraphs—up to you) the ones that come to mind.

Then, choose one of these situations. Ideally, a fairly specific, medium-size one should be selected (for example, getting overwhelmed about a particular task or situation at work). That's your MOMF focus for this chapter.

Once Tab came to believe that, yep, a need to control was a problem for her, she decided to try out MOMF on a medium-size situation that she was handling with control-freaking. (The holiday shit show was a ninja-level issue—she was going to have to work up to that.)

Every other week, Tab was in charge of coordinating the hospitality (coffee, snacks, setup, cleanup) for coffee hour after services at her church. It had become something she felt trapped in and had started to hate doing. But she did not feel able to stop doing it.

First, she did the inner control freak exercise, spending some time with her journal writing about her core beliefs, self-talk, life experiences, and personality traits. She also wrote about how they contributed to her

#*@&*!!

deeply fucked-up relationship to her volunteer commitment. She got some insights into how and why she ended up in this situation.

Then Tab went to work on the CBT, mindfulness, second arrow, and MOMF angles. First, she created some evidence-based counter-statements for her self-talk. "I can't ever stop doing it—there isn't anybody else" was countered by "I don't know that there's no one unless I ask. That's how I started—I got asked." And "It's easier to keep doing this than try to find someone else" was countered by "It'll be hard for a while to find and help train and support someone else, but it will sure as shit be easier than to keep doing this with no end in sight." Tab started making a list of people she'd try asking when she was ready.

Next, Tab started a practice of five minutes of mindful sitting every morning to begin building her skills. When her anxious, overwhelmed, resentful feelings surfaced (usually the Saturday before her volunteer shift), she practiced sitting still and noticing her thoughts and feelings, and letting them pass. She journaled about it too—ten minutes on Sunday mornings when her anxiety was high, then ten minutes more after she got home from church, when she felt relieved but also resentful and used up.

Then she looked at her journal for pieces of self-talk that she could a) do counterstatements for, and b) use to practice not picking up the second arrow of shaming herself for her thoughts and feelings. "It is what it is," she told herself. "It's just my old shit. I know where it's coming from, and I'm starting to deal with it."

When it was time to start looking for someone else to take one of her Sundays each month, Tab was terrified but determined. She got the word out that coffee hour needed a new volunteer or two, let people know when she was stopping, and then showed up at coffee hour armed with her MOMF tools. First, she took a deep breath and acknowledged her big feelings: "There are those fucked-up feelings again. They don't mean anything." Then Tab affirmed her right to be herself: "I embrace my flawed inner motherfucker!"

The first day was a lot of work, and Tab had to use every tool she had. But it got easier. And she got to see that the world didn't end, and nobody got hurt, when she allowed herself to just show up and not be in control. She was still a caring part of her church community—and inwardly as salty as shit whenever she needed to be.

She started getting some ideas about next Thanksgiving…

Make a MOMF Plan

Time to start letting go of the banana you identified in the previous exercise—your medium-size control-freak scenario—and getting ready to build some MOMF skills.

In your journal, repeat the scenario on a fresh page (for example, "Trying to micromanage what my daughter wears to school").

Choose a time frame for your experiment—a week, two weeks, a month, whatever you think will give you some time to see how it goes. Write this down too. Then answer the following questions in your journal:

CBT: What self-talk do you want to make counterstatements for?

Mindfulness: What parts of your situation will benefit from your holding an open mind and noticing what's happening inside you and outside you?

MOMF: What salty mantras, affirmations, rhymes, haiku, or clapbacks can you use when you need to check yourself at the moment when you are about to act like a motherfucker?

Second arrow: What's the thing you do that makes this scenario worse for yourself? How are you going to put it down the next time you go to stab yourself with it? (CBT, mindfulness, and MOMF tools can all help—mix it up until you find what works for you.)

Once you've worked the plan for the amount of time you chose for the experiment, assess and retool. What's working? What needs tweaking? What's next?

WHY CONTROL IS THE PROBLEM, NOT THE SOLUTION

I believe that the drive to control comes from anxiety and the desire to avoid negative feelings. Our brain is wired to foresee what threats lie ahead so that we can get ready to problem-solve. For control junkies, the self-talk is, "If I can get ahead of the problems in my life, I can avoid them." We believe that in this way we can feel safe. Life will feel predictable, and therefore, we hope and believe, we can feel more relaxed. The belief that we actually have control over much of what happens around us is an illusion, so we're doomed to fail. But we still try.

It's not just the situations we're in that we try to control. Au contraire, my friend. Way too much of the time it's our own feelings. I'd even argue there's a movement in American culture of people seeking to be in a constant state of happiness. We see our doctors after the death of a loved one or loss of a job seeking a pill to feel better. It's as if we have the expectation that we shouldn't feel bad, or we must feel better quickly. This drives addiction, too: alcohol and drugs, shopping and spending, relationships, gambling—all these are ways to try to feel good.

Chasing good feelings is doomed to fail, just so you know. No one succeeds at this for more than a little while. Partly this is because we can't ever truly know happiness and peace if we haven't also experienced sadness, shame, anger, guilt… We *have* to feel bad when bad things happen, or it becomes impossible to feel good when the time is right.

#*@&*!!

In his poem "The Guest House,"[10] the thirteenth-century Persian poet Jalaluddin Rumi suggests that we should welcome all emotions as visitors because they are transient. Allowing them to arrive and depart, we can study and know them. Mindfulness teaches us how to sit with our emotions and stop judging them as good or bad. When we use mindfulness, we let our emotions come and go without trying to fix them.

Your feelings are there to inform you about your situation. Your job is not to rush to change them but to figure out what you need to understand, what you need to tolerate, what you can change, and what you need to MOMF from.

You may be confused at this point. In the section on CBT in chapter 1, I advised you to identify your negative thoughts and argue with them *in order to improve how you are feeling*. Now I am suggesting that you shouldn't rush to change them but should just sit with your emotions and accept them.

Both are right, *depending on the context*, which is why I suggest both strategies. We need to take time and sit with our emotions so that we can understand them. In times of grief and loss, there is nothing to argue with or fix, so we can just let the feelings come and go. In other situations, our pain may be self-inflicted because we are beating ourselves up with negative thinking. In those circumstances, we must work to change the irrational thoughts that are driving the feelings.

I remember hearing a story on the radio several years ago. Folks were asked the question, "If you were offered a pill that could take away your pain after a breakup, would you take the pill?" My first reaction was, "No way! If I took a pill, I wouldn't learn how to stop doing the same stupid shit." My next reaction was, "Come on, fucker, be real. You'd take the pill in a heartbeat." The intensity of heartbreak pushes us to do anything to avoid it, but avoidance isn't always the best thing.

#*@&*!!

Is it better to live life trying to limit the range of emotions, or to fully understand and know what it feels like to be on the highest high compared with the lowest low?

The takeaway is this: be mindful of reality and accept it, rather than try to pretend it is something different. It is also this: accept that it isn't up to you or me to fix everything. We just end up appearing to be the craziest fuckers of all for expecting people and situations to be what they are not.

When we try too hard to control the insanity around us because we think we know what is best, we can miss the opportunity to see in new ways and experience new things. Consider this: If, as a child, you ever went on a family or school trip that involved a long car ride, you may remember that all you wanted to do was get there. All you could think about was what you would do once you arrived. But when you grew up, maybe what you remember the most was the circus going on in the car—the ride, sibling fights, your parents' threats while trying to reach into the backseat, and the togetherness you experienced under stressful circumstances.

Letting go of control is about letting things unfold the way they are supposed to and trusting that things will work out. We don't always have the answers that we think we have. Take a leap of faith. Go with the flow. Say to yourself, "Fuck it." Watch your life with excitement and curiosity to see what crazy things will happen next. Worry less about judging things as good or bad. You may even start to see the humor in the unlikeliest situations.

Map Your Emotion-Control Habits

In what situations do you try to avoid, change, or otherwise control your emotions? Write about this in your journal.

#*@&*!!

Which emotions do you tend to clamp down on or wiggle away from the most?

The next time a tough emotional situation comes up, ask yourself mindfully, "What fears and self-talk are trying to make me dodge, deflect, deny, or act out to manage my emotions?"

When you are working so hard to escape or control your emotions, what's the second arrow you're stabbing yourself with?

What tools or strategies could you use to change the unhelpful ways you cope with your emotions?

FLIPPING THE SCRIPT ON SHAME TALK

One day I was taking a walk with my preteen son after he had just gotten into trouble for some misdeed. He emphatically stated, "Mom, when I grow up, I hope I never make any mistakes." I responded, "Well, I hope you make a ton of mistakes. My wish for you is that you mess up all over the place, because that is how you will learn so much about yourself and the world."

Mistakes do come with pain, and the pain teaches us to change our patterns of behavior. To a point.

When the pain becomes chronic shame, it's no longer useful. When we hold on to it, shame becomes a mean, sadistic emotion that cuts to our core. When you make a mistake, your job is to focus on the behavior and what went wrong, and to do the repairs. When shame takes over, it can make you feel like *you* are the mistake. Not only is "I am the mistake" both an unfixable problem and a goddamn lie, but it also distracts you from doing the real work of acknowledging the mistake and trying to make amends. You're too wrapped up in stabbing yourself with how bad you suck. This is how shame wrecks relationships and lives.

I am not saying that there are no situations when shame isn't appropriate. For example, if I intentionally terrify a child, I should feel

ashamed. If I harm another person on purpose, I should feel ashamed. Like any emotion, shame has a message: you fucked up. But shame is often a mislearned emotion, so that what you hear is "You *are* fucked up." Not helpful.

A shame-based belief filter ("I am wrong/bad/the problem") gets locked in when we're children. When you make mistakes as a child or misbehave, you may have learned that it's not the behavior but *you* that is a problem. Chronic shame can also come from experiences of childhood abuse. The shame filter delivers the deeply flawed emotional message that there is something really wrong within you that cannot be fixed.

I hate the shame filter. It is the true inner motherfucker. It hijacks people's lives without any understandable reason. I am not sure that the shame filter can ever be eradicated once it's in place. But it can be fought—and even defanged.

MOMF tools are perfect for handling a shame attack. Reframing shameful self-talk and coming up with counterstatements (CBT) is a natural shame-buster, because shame says the most wrong-headed, crazy-ass things. Statements like "I am the worst!" and "I can't ever be trusted" are pretty easy to find evidence against (unless you are literally Charles Manson). Practicing mindful noticing (mindfulness) around our shameful self-talk allows us to let it come up and fade away, rather than setting up camp and digging a moat around our hearts. Shame thoughts are the ultimate second arrow, because they keep us from making the real repairs for the actual damage we may have caused. And if ever there was a motherfucker who needed to move the fuck on, it's shame talk.

If some of your strongest self-talk says things like "I'm the worst" or "I suck" or "I can't ever let anyone see what I'm really like," you've probably got a shame belief filter interfering between you and the real world

#*@&*!!

in front of you. You might want to do some journaling or reading about shame (see the recommended reading section at the back of the book), because the more space you can put between your actual self (who does not suck and is not the worst) and your shame stories, the better chance you have of kicking shame to the curb.

To shut down shame when it's trying to hijack your daily life, start by fencing it in with CBT, letting it flow through with mindfulness, and then shutting it down with sass. You might say to yourself, "Shit happened, and I feel so bad about it. I feel like I fucked it up, and like I'll always fuck it up, because I am a fuckup. That's my shame filter, and it's not letting me see the situation for what it is. I won't let it make me helpless, because I'm not." Or you could say, "Huh, I'm noticing shame. It feels like X in my body, and it's telling me Y and Z." Or "Sweetheart, I love your crazy ass, but you need to drop that pile of horseshit right now."

MOMF Like a Mofo

- **Try a daily affirmation focused on letting go of control.** Get an app that sends you a thought or a reminder, and MOMF it up. Consciously repeat the affirmation throughout the day. Each time you catch yourself trying to control, yell, "Fuck that! I'm a free motherfucker!" And when you catch yourself engaging in self-talk around trying to be perfect, yell, "Fuck the monkey!" Get up and exercise or get your mind on something else.

- **Review your journal for negative beliefs and self-talk themes around control or shame.** Make this your focus for a week. Write some MOMF counterstatements that include acceptance and transcendence ("You're not psychic, motherfucker. Let's see where this is going before you try to change it." "It is just the way it is—situation normal, all fucked up.").

#*@&*!!

CHAPTER 4

When Your Love Life Is Wrecking You

Relationship issues are among the most common reasons people seek my help. When humans get together, there is generally going to be some trouble. We can accept that and work through it. We can learn to better understand ourselves and our partners. We can grow together, support, compromise, keep working. We're all grown-ups, right? We've got this.

Eh, maybe not so much.

Sooner or later, more often than not, my patients ask some version of the classic question: "How do I get so-and-so to change?" And there it is. People seek help with their romantic relationships because they want me to help them fix or change, or at least influence or persuade, the other person so that the relationship will work better. And when we do a little digging, it's usually not the other person's behavior they want to change. Not really. They want to change the other person's personality—that is, the deep core of the person that's been shaped by genetics and life experience since before they were even born.

Yeah, I'm not that good. No one is.

In this chapter, I'm going to walk you through a set of common relationship traps with a goal of getting you freer to make relationship choices like a grown-ass motherfucker.

Sri and Paul's Story

Sri and Paul had been married for five years when they came to see me. They were miserable. They seemed to fight about everything. Paul thought Sri was hypercritical and controlling. Sri thought Paul was a selfish bastard who always did his own thing and left her to do all the work.

When I asked Sri and Paul how they met and what they found attractive about each other, Sri said that Paul was outgoing and had a lot of enthusiasm for life. He was always doing something spontaneous and fun, and she enjoyed hearing about his adventures. Paul said he'd admired how Sri had her life together—she knew what she wanted and how to get it. She was also a great listener.

Now, though, Sri hated that Paul "couldn't commit" to decisions. She hated that Paul was so social that he never wanted to be at home with her. Paul resented that Sri "wanted to control everything," and he felt like nothing he did met her standards. And they were both confused because they were being who they always were, but now the other person was irritated by things that used to seem fine. They'd been so much in love. What happened?

In Sri and Paul I recognized a familiar story: what had originally been attractive to the other person had become offensive.

WHEN IT'S NOT CUTE ANYMORE

People don't tend to like it when I tell them that if they want to improve their relationship, they will need to accept who the other person is at their core—their personality and their beliefs. They don't have to adore it, just really accept it with no expectation that the person will change.

In this case, Sri and Paul had *always* been really different from one another. In the beginning, they each liked that. But somewhere along the way, each had developed an expectation that the other person would change as they made a new life together.

The self-talk of people in conflicted relationships often takes this form: "If she loved me, she would change her ways." Also, "I'm clearly right. If he would just admit that he is wrong, we could fix this."

Underlying this may be the belief that successful romantic relationships "should be easy" or "should always be happy." In reality, relationships take a lot of work, and although happiness is important, it is not reasonable to think you will always be happy. These expectations are self-defeating.

If we cling to our self-righteousness, this interferes with seeing that the other person is just being who they've always been. Resentment and anger grow, and it is easy to begin to see nothing other than negative.

Q: Once again, what's not going to automatically change?

A: Your personality and the distorted ways you see the world. Also, your partner's personality and beliefs.

Whatever solution there is to the situation, a good chunk of it is in your hands, my friend. There are things you need to accept and things you can work with.

The first part of relationship management is being honest with yourself so you can make clear decisions. Your relationship cannot be a fairy tale, and your partner cannot be the prince or princess you might have created in your mind. You need to identify your own inappropriate expectations and negative self-talk, and hold yourself accountable for the role you play when things aren't working.

#*@&*!!

What Used to Be Okay But Isn't Now?

Think about, write about, and—if possible—talk to your partner about:

- The things that you're holding against your partner that are likely personality related. Think especially of things that you have known about from the beginning and maybe used to think were cute, or that you like in some situations but can't stand in others.

- The negative things you say to yourself about your partner that fuels resentment.

How might you challenge your beliefs and counter your self-talk when it pops up?

RELATIONSHIP TRAP #1: RECAPITULATION

It's interesting when people know what their problem is and hate the feeling associated with the problem but still make choices that re-create the problem over and over. Some psychologists call this "recapitulation." People keep engaging in scenarios over and over, hoping they'll get it right or somehow fix the core issue. Here is an example:

A woman who saw her father abusing her mother vowed, "I will never be with a man like my father." Of course, she found herself dating men just like her father. Why is that? Is it because she wants to be with abusive men? No! Fuck that. It's because humans are subconsciously drawn to qualities in others that remind us of unresolved issues. Without really being aware of what we're doing, we use current relationships to reenact childhood scenarios and fix what we couldn't fix in our parents or in other important role models. As a professor of mine used to put it, some spooky shit happens in the human psyche.

The CBT folks think that we repeat patterns because of mistaken or distorted beliefs (such as "This is what people do. They fight."). This is part of it, but there are other, more deeply emotional undercurrents to this pattern: it's familiar to us.

It could also be that people, in general, just have a hard time changing or being different. And sometimes the pain associated with a known path seems more inviting—or at least more bearable—than the potential pain associated with an unknown path. Nothing you don't already know. Change is hard.

The bottom line: many of us are just not actively aware when we are in these situations. It's worth considering what part unawareness of old patterns—or fear of new ones—is playing in your relationship issues.

Your Relationship Beliefs

Is your love life like Groundhog Day? That is, do you think you might be recapitulating? Go back to the two exercises in chapter 1: "What's Your Belief Filter?" and "What Are Your Core Beliefs?" What do you find there that might be feeding your relationship pain? Journal about what you think the connections are.

If you like, you can work through those exercises again, focusing on your beliefs about what relationships are for. How do you think you are "supposed" to be in a relationship? How is your partner "supposed" to be, according to your belief filters?

RELATIONSHIP TRAP #2: THE RABBIT HOLE OF WHY

When trying to understand yourself in relationships, it's sooooooo tempting to ask why. Why didn't things work out? Why does the other person not want to be with me? Why does the other person treat me

badly? "Why" is so often the entrance to an endless rabbit hole, and diving into it won't get you anywhere you want or need to be.

The underlying question of this particular sad rabbit hole of why seems to be, "What is wrong with me?" I think there are two responses to this question.

The first response is that *both* parties have a role in relationship failures. It is not about there being something unlovable or undesirable about *you*. This kind of thinking is a distraction—an invitation to a truly worthless pity party.

The follow-up response is a question: Why would you want to force something to work that causes you such pain? You can *choose* how you understand and react to a relationship falling apart. You do this by trying to be curious and mindful about it.

Being mindful will not erase the disappointment and grief that comes with a relationship ending, but you can stop yourself from rethinking and replaying scenarios over and over. It's the rumination that is torture. With acceptance, you will at least not be amping up your pain through your own actions. You will allow yourself to move on, motherfucker.

Getting Past "Why (Not) Me?"

If you find yourself pinning the blame for your relationship pain on your innate unlovability, or if you just can't stop ruminating, it's time to MOMF. Identify the negative self-talk, hold yourself accountable for wasting time on it, and find something else to do. In your journal, map out and fight back at each piece of negative self-talk that's tormenting you. Use this format:

1.   My negative self-talk: _____.

2.   This super unhelpful message comes from my core belief or belief filter that: _____.

#*@&*!!

3.   This self-talk is a waste of time, and every time I notice it popping up, I'm going to _____.

Just RSVP "Hell no" to the pity party.

If your relationship is failing or has failed, a mindfulness perspective can help you understand and truly accept that maybe it wasn't meant to be. When negative self-talk has you in its jaws, take a mindful moment to feel your body and breath, and to notice your thoughts and feelings, and then let them go. Every little moment of mindful curiosity and acceptance you can manage will loosen the grip of why.

RELATIONSHIP TRAP #3: UNHEALTHY CODEPENDENCE

What is one of the biggest obstacles to moving on from messed-up relationships? In my opinion, it's unhealthy codependence.

Unfortunately, the term "codependence" has gotten a certain rep over the years because it's been associated with relationships whereby one or both partners are substance abusers. Really, all human beings have the capacity to be at least somewhat codependent (except maybe sociopaths). We are wired to need each other and to try to influence the behavior of the people we're in relationship with.

Unhealthy codependence tends to happen when our actions are aimed to fix, control, or manipulate another person. Sometimes we find ourselves in codependent situations we didn't see coming. Other times it's a repeated pattern of behavior—wherever we go and whoever we're with, there's codependence.

Here's an example of how it looks.

One person (let's call her Meri) *overfunctions* (does too much) to help, protect, or fix another person (let's call her Sally). Sally comes to rely on Meri to function (this is *overreliance*). Sally *underfunctions* in

#*@&*!!

parts of her life where she should be able to deal. Meri's the fixer, Sally's the fixee.

Meri, like a typical fixer, likes to control situations. And she generally has good intentions. However, by doing too much, she doesn't allow the other person to learn to solve her own problems.

Sally is happy enough to let Meri be in control. She might be lazy or anxious or shy or just someone who avoids conflict, so it's easier for her to just go along. For whatever reason, the situation is working for her. However, by not stepping up to full equal adult status, she doesn't really grow as a person. She gets more helpless. Her self-esteem goes into the toilet.

In fact, low self-esteem is at the heart of a lot of unhealthy codependent relationships. Fixers feel more important or powerful when they can help or fix. Fixees' low self-esteem convinces them to allow others to try and fix them. It seems like an amazing fit in the beginning, and that is why so many romantic relationships are codependent.

Conflict boils up more for the fixers, who often feel resentful because they are doing all of the work and feel unappreciated. They have a hard time changing their own behavior—or even believing that it's possible for them to change. The *other* person needs to change first. Then they wouldn't *have to* do all this extra stuff that their partner isn't dealing with. The fixer has a problem because the fixee *is a* problem.

Ouch.

Codependent Gender Roles?

A lot of codependent conflict seems to come from people's gender roles. See if this rings a bell: Woman goes to man to share her problems, frustrations, and concerns. Man jumps in to enlighten with insight, guidance, and problem solving. Woman gets angry because she didn't ask for "the answer." She just wanted the man to listen. Man gets angry because he feels like the woman asked for help and then rejected it.

Feeling like we have the answer for someone else when that person has not asked for a solution is judgmental. It's like saying that we think the other person isn't bright enough to come up with the solution on their own. On the other hand, dumping a whole lot of problem-talk on someone without telling them ahead of time what we want from the conversation is also a bullshit move. By whatever mixture of nature and nurture, lots of men tend to problem-solve, while women tend to share feelings. Both are trying to show care and connection, and both are blowing it, big-time.

Let's look at a few more examples of codependence from my practice.

Sharene + All Her Boyfriends: "I Have Some Notes." Sharene kept meeting men who didn't live up to their potential. This wasn't what she said she wanted in a partner, but it was a pattern. She would meet a man, fall in love, identify several things he could do to improve, and start working very hard to help him become a better person. Long story short: those guys never went the distance somehow, and Sharene, disappointed, was off to find her next project.

Bart + Monzelle: A Bottomless Pit. Bart was in a committed relationship with Monzelle. Monzelle's truest partner was her own crappy self-esteem. She was convinced (on no evidence) that Bart was cheating on her. Over and over, they had a conversation during which Bart tried to convince Monzelle that he wasn't cheating. He let her review his emails and look at his texts and call logs. He felt obligated to dote on Monzelle, telling her how beautiful and desirable she was just to make her feel okay for a while. It used to feel so romantic. He used to love feeling like the strong, sweet, kind boyfriend. Now it just felt like a

#*@&*!!

full-time job—the kind where you work your ass off and still hardly make enough to pay the bills.

Kurt + Spencer: A Long Cold War. Kurt felt like he was doing all the work around the house, including dinner preparation, laundry, house-work, and childcare. He felt unappreciated and resentful. Spencer, his spouse, was willing to pitch in and help out when he got around to it, which generally wasn't on Kurt's timeline—or to Kurt's standards. Kurt often went ahead and did the things he'd asked Spencer to do, because even if Spencer got around to it, Kurt was never happy with the outcome.

Spencer made his schedule according to his own needs: playing cards, playing golf, yard work on the weekends. Basically, if he wanted or needed time, he took it—usually without checking first with his spouse. Kurt felt unable to make his own plans—he was always too busy to take time for himself. Kurt put his life on hold, becoming ever more angry and resentful. Spencer was angry because his spouse was always criticizing and nagging him. They never went out on dates and mainly fought about what needed to be done around the house.

Advice Columnist Time!

Let's switch it up for a minute and focus on someone else's problems. Pick one (or more!) of the relationships above (Sharene + Boyfriend, Bart + Monzelle, or Kurt + Spencer) and imagine one of these people is writing to you, an advice columnist, for relationship help. Imagine you are the kind of columnist who gives real help and advice, and imagine also that they really want to do what it takes to have a happy, healthy romantic relationship.

In your journal, write their question first, then write your answer. Use the tools and concepts you've encountered in this book.

Bonus round: If you picked a fixer to advise, do it again, but this time with a fixee.

#*@&*!!

WORKABLE, UNWORKABLE, OR STRAIGHT-UP TOXIC?

Once we get real with ourselves about our relationships, we are able to better see whether we are being unreasonable about what we want. Where can we do some work that will really help?

Sometimes we decide that a relationship is unsatisfying enough that we (or our partner) call it quits. It's unworkable, and we end it.

Sometimes what we come to see is that the relationship is actually toxic. By toxic, I mean a range of things. It can refer to abuse (verbal, emotional, physical), but "toxic" can also just be a label for other kinds of unhealthiness. I consider a relationship toxic when one or both people repeatedly engage in behaviors that are hurtful and damaging.

This goes way beyond having disagreements or being irritated with one another.

It's a pattern, a current, a way of relating that hurts and that we can't seem to move beyond. We're stuck in it, and it sucks.

Toxic relationships make us feel sick and beaten down. They even impair our ability to function. If we are honest with ourselves and acknowledge that our relationship is toxic, we literally need to move on, motherfucker. Walk away. This is the bottom line, the part for which we are accountable to ourselves. And it's easier said than done.

Mimi's Story

When we met, Mimi was a hard worker in a stable job and was pretty put together. Mimi was having a difficult time breaking it off with Roy, who was clearly unable to commit to a healthy relationship. Mimi and Roy would break up, but then she would text or call him when she felt lonely. They'd get back together, and then they would break up again. This time Mimi would avoid contact, but

then Roy would end up calling or texting her, and she'd get hooked in again. The cycle had been going on for almost a year.

Mimi acknowledged that Roy was damaged. She also listed the ways the relationship was messed up: he would accuse her of ghosting, drinking too much, and avoiding commitment; he called her names like "bitch," "dumbass," and "fat ass"; interactions with him left her convinced that she must be a bad person; and Mimi's friends and family hated Roy and constantly told her she deserved better.

Mimi believed that she deserved more, but she also believed that she could fix Roy. Her self-talk was, "Roy is a good person inside. I've seen it. I just have to help him be that person."

Mimi felt so much better when Roy wasn't around. She could see it clearly, and she agreed with me that the relationship needed to end, because the cycle of breakups and makeups was making her more and more sad. She acknowledged that she knew she could end the relationship, but she didn't feel in control.

We worked on the problem using CBT. We reviewed the evidence, including incidents when Roy treated her disrespectfully and hurtfully, and times when Roy wasn't reliable. We worked on counterstatements, such as, "Roy is choosing to be cruel to me." "I cannot make him into the person I want him to be." "He is not the person I want."

We also worked on her self-care, emphasizing her habits of exercising and journaling. When I asked Mimi to be mindful of her emotions—to let them come and go—she said this was overwhelming, but she agreed to try it for three minutes at a time, to build her skill slowly. She had already identified that her negative self-talk was a major problem, but she hadn't yet been able to overcome it. I urged her to notice it, counter it, and let it go.

I told Mimi to focus on changing her behavior and to avoid all contact: block Roy's phone numbers, texts, and emails; stay away

#*@&*!!

from all sad movies and songs; and not talk to his family. I especially told her not to drink, because when people drink, they can
become overly emotional and drunk-dial. For her, it was in moments
of drunkenness that past makeups occurred. I told her to journal
instead of drinking. (You know that at this point she was thinking
what a bitch I was.)

Mimi agreed to this plan more than once. Because (somehow)
there would be contact, which was always (somehow) out of her
control. There was a family tragedy. Roy needed her for something
that only she could do. That sort of thing. Once she agreed to talk
to him, he would admit his fault. This fed into the self-talk that Roy
needed her for help, and Mimi would become overwhelmed with
guilt and sadness. I told Mimi that Roy had to keep checking that
she was lusting for him because it made him feel important. She
could see this pattern too, and that was a start.

One day, Mimi came in, head hung low, saying Roy had, once
again, made contact after a long separation. She was demoralized.
She couldn't stop thinking about him. It was the same story. Mimi
insisted that I give her something that would force her to get over
him. (If only I was that brilliant.) She got out her tablet, ready to
take notes.

I felt like I was empty. I had given her a fuck-ton of tools.
There was nothing left to say.

Perhaps it was her sad eyes, so I dug deeper. We hadn't yet tried
MOMF, and I decided to present it as the answer.

I said, "Okay. Next time you start thinking about him, say to
yourself, 'Move on, motherfucker.'"

I told her to use this phrase to jolt herself into the reality that
she has some control over the situation. I told her she was being a
motherfucker, and she could laugh or cry about it. It was her choice.

#*@&*!!

She smiled. She looked me right in the eye and said she'd give it a try. She wrote it down and left.

When Mimi came back, she was on fire. "Every time I catch myself thinking about the past and the good times, I say to myself, 'Move on, motherfucker!'" It was working. Not every time and not perfectly, but it did jolt her out of her fantasy that she could fix it if she just tried again, more, harder. She could even laugh about the fantasy—a little.

That was the core issue, by the way. Mimi kept trying to make it work because she wanted to be with the person she had fantasized that her ex-boyfriend was instead of the jackass he actually was when he was with her. Roy had such potential! It was up to her to help him reach it! Also, she had spent so many years trying to make it happen that it seemed like it would be a waste to stop. It was kind of like that nagging feeling that you shouldn't walk away from the slot machine in case it is about ready to pay out. Never mind that Roy's "potential" didn't even live in the same country as reality. Mimi became able to come back to reality, where she was acting like a motherfucker—chasing after an abusive ex-boyfriend frog that she pretended was a prince. The happiest possible ending turned out to be moving the fuck on.

When people overfunction in unworkable or toxic relationships, it is often because they tell themselves sad stories: the other person needs them, the other person can't do it alone, things will go so badly if they don't step in.

Believing those stories is the second arrow—we are choosing to hurt ourselves in those moments. Believing something in spite of evidence and experience is a *choice*. Imagining worst-case scenarios, and rushing to save others from them, is a choice. Believing self-defeating, sad stories like "I don't deserve better," "This is all I have," or "Things won't be better with anyone else" is also a choice.

What's Your Sad Story?

Meditate, journal, or reflect on the following: What sad or fearful or self-deluding stories do you tell yourself? If you can identify the moment you stab yourself with the second arrow, you have found the place where you can make a different choice. And this does *not need* to mean leaving the relationship. Often, it just means a behavior, belief, or other choice that is hurting, not helping.

Should You Stay or Should You Go?

Bad relationship patterns are hard to change. It is difficult to walk away from relationships, even when they are really unhealthy. Often, couples have to completely destroy anything good that is left in order to move on. We stay until the bitter end and even beyond—to the point that we grow to hate the other person and ourselves. We just don't leave. Sometimes we become so accustomed to dysfunction that we can't see how much it's wrecking us.

My patients talk about feeling sluggish, unhappy, unfulfilled—yet they don't want to leave the relationship that they themselves identify as sick-making. Choosing to stay in such a relationship makes *you* the motherfucker in the scenario.

If you decide to stay in a dysfunctional relationship, you can still move on. You must, actually: you MOMF from the same complaints and the same fights. As the saying goes, you change what you can (including your own behavior), accept what you can't, and actively practice figuring out which is which.

#*@&*!!

You accept and let go in order to make the relationship work, or you literally MOMF from the relationship because you don't want to remain in it, stabbing yourself over and over with the second arrow. You have to choose a path and not behave like a victim who has no choices. There are always choices, including the choice to stay in an unhappy relationship for reality-based reasons, like parenting or finances.

You must decide what you do want instead of what you don't want. You make the change you have been waiting for. You can discover that you are your own savior any time you are ready. It's incredibly powerful to realize that you're the motherfucker in charge, able to focus on what you can control—your behavior.

I guarantee you that workable, good, and great relationships come in a billion different flavors. All of them benefit from the MOMF principles of being real, laughing hard, and owning your choices.

What Are Your Pain Points?

Journal on these questions:

What would you like to change about your romantic relationship? Focus particularly on what you bring to the situation.

When do you pick up the second arrow? For example, is it your own negative self-talk or how you put up with bad behavior?

What is your biggest fear about relationships? Would you survive if it came true? What evidence do you have to support your conclusions?

Now make a list of what *must* change in order for you to take control of your happiness. Important: These are changes *you* can make. They do *not* depend on the other person changing a single thing. What steps are necessary to make the list a reality? What will get in the way? How will you handle that? Is there anything you need to make your plan a success?

#*@&*!!

MOMF Like a Mofo

- **Ask a friend for feedback on your codependent tendencies.** Friends are great sources of feedback on our patterns of behavior. Ask your friends what else they notice about your relationship choices. If you think you have unhealthy codependent patterns, check out Co-Dependents Anonymous (http://CoDA.org).

- **Keep journaling for fifteen minutes a day.** Notice times when you might be trying to fix things for others. How can you change the focus to what you can do for yourself? If you find catastrophic self-talk, counter it by saying, "I need to let others grow through their pain. [Person] deserves to grow too."

- **Make a list of salty counterstatements to use when arguing your negative self-talk patterns and codependent tendencies.** ("Motherfucker, you can only control your own behaviors. If you don't like how things are going, make the change you want.") Make a list of salty affirmations that you can use to pump yourself up when you are feeling like going back to your old ways, or you are feeling low about change ("Breathe in strength. Breathe out bullshit."). Practice all of these to make them a habit.

- **Distract yourself.** Make a list of activities (like exercising or calling a friend) you can do when your thoughts are getting the best of you.

#*@&*!!

CHAPTER 5

When You're Sure You're Screwing Up Your Kids

Let's be real.

For a lot of us, the time we spend analyzing ourselves and what went wrong in our own life journey is dwarfed by the time we spend wondering how much damage we are doing to our kids.

We try so hard. And there is a mountain of rules, advice, recommendations, warnings, and attitudes from friends, relatives, random strangers, and experts spewing out an infinity of books, articles, videos, and programs to "help" us. Everyone and their mom has an opinion that they think is a fact. The recommendations change all the time, and people are always arguing about them. Parenting is the most important thing most of us ever do in life, and there seems to be no way to get it right.

Hear me clearly say, "Fuck that!" The truth about parenting is: we all do the best we can, and most of the time it's good enough. When we let anxious self-talk ("I'm screwing up my child" or "What if I screw up my child?") and unhelpful emotions (like toxic levels of guilt and shame) drive the bus, we are on the road to crazy town.

Do you find yourself grappling with "not good enough" self-talk around parenting? Do you worry excessively about saying and doing the right things? Then this chapter is for you.

Here, we'll work on some tools and perspective-taking that'll help you get off that crazy bus and do the only thing you need to do to be a good-enough parent (aside from keeping them fed, housed, and safe): be present in your kids' lives and love them.

Truly, that's it.

Yes, there absolutely are some parenting no-no's, namely abuse (verbal, emotional, or physical) and neglect (not meeting your child's basic needs). Just know that you have to consistently screw up as a parent in some big ways to do lasting damage. Most of the time, you will know how to do a good-enough job.

Basically, throughout your decades of parenting, there will be times when you'll battle fear-driven self-talk and overprotection, or guilt-driven overcompensation, and that's what we'll deal with here.

Before we start: I'm not here to judge your style or your choices. There are a shit-ton of different parenting styles, and we all make our best choices based on our values. If any of my parenting opinions don't fit for you, then tell me to fuck off. Just know your kids and love them. And give yourself a break.

THERE IS NO PERFECT PARENT

The responsibility and consequences of parenting are beyond comprehension. We just know we don't want to screw up our kids. Even if we had a good parenting role model, each generation brings new challenges. (I won't list the challenges here: your news and social media feeds tell you all about them every day.)

#*@&*!!

That's why "There is no perfect parent" is the first rule of Parent Club. If you think you've spotted one in your community, that's just because you don't have enough information. Every last one of us is sometimes just a clown in a feral cat rodeo.

Despite what you might think, my kids still don't know how much I cuss. It is a private pleasure. Anyway, my family and I were in Lake Buena Vista, Florida, for a Disney trip a couple of years ago. We rented a car and were up early to drive to the parks. In front of the hotel was a busy four-lane road. I was obviously not entirely alert, and I turned the wrong way on a one-way street. Luckily, it was early enough that there wasn't much traffic. I yelled, "Fuck!" In the back seat, my youngest screamed with glee, "So that is what 'the F word' stands for!" A few weeks later, my older son comes to me on a Sunday when we had a friend over. He says to me, "Mom, Harrie is teaching Max the F word." Yes, people pay me to help them with their problems, including parenting. And I'm a role model for human parenting limitations.

Here's another true story.

When I was about ten or eleven, I hit a patch of loose gravel and wrecked my bike. My left knee still has a purplish/blackish scar in the shape of skid marks. I've always called it my dirty knee. My recollection is that I went inside the house crying after the accident. I begged my mother to take me to the hospital and get stitches, but my mother was too busy to mess with me. I carry the scar as a result, and this is a very clear memory for me. When you ask my mom, she has a different recollection. She says that she tried to clean out my wound with a wet washcloth, but I resisted. I was screaming and yelling bloody murder, and there was nothing she could do for me. Knowing the characters involved, I absolutely believe my mother despite my strong memory of something entirely different.

#*@&*!!

My point? You can be a good parent and do the right thing, and your children may still hold it against you. There is no way to escape childhood without some kind of baggage. Any terrible, guilt-ridden stories that you tell yourself about how you have done all the wrong things as a parent are a complete waste of time.

Our guilty stories are the second arrow, because not only do they get in the way of our being present in our children's lives, but there may also be zero relationship between what really happened and what is remembered anyway.

The Worst Parent Ever?

What stories are you telling yourself about screwing up your kids that are making you anxious, sad, or miserable? These could be stories you tell yourself over and over again, or stories that come from a painful incident.

How are your belief filter and your core beliefs affecting these stories?

What's the evidence you use to support these stories? (Remember, if your "evidence" is "X parent I know who would never fuck up like that," that's bullshit. X parent you know is literally fucking up all over the place.) How can you counter it?

CONDITIONS OF WORTH

Carl Rogers,[11] one of the fathers of humanistic psychology, talked about "conditions of worth" as a big part of low self-esteem. As someone who works with adults still trying to recover from their childhoods, I see this all the time. *Conditions of worth* are direct and indirect messages we send to our children as they develop. We say or imply, "You are worthwhile if _____."

You could fill that blank line with "if you don't talk back," "if you pick up after yourself," "if you make good grades," "if you are a star athlete," and so on. Most of the time, the messages aren't spoken but learned through parents' praise or criticism. Children internalize these messages, and at some point they no longer need the parent to be the messenger. The children start to tell themselves, "I am worthwhile if _____." Unfortunately, it can be very hard—if not impossible—to get rid of these conditions of worth once they enter a kid's belief system.

It's really hard for parents not to do this to our kids at least some of the time. We love them so much that we want to "make" them better. Part of our job, of course, is to teach them values. And we can't help wanting good things for them in their lives.

It is *how* we teach values and provide good things that are important. If we can keep hold of the idea that no habits or skills or accomplishments are more valuable than our child's heart or our bond with them, we can steer a good-enough course. We can encourage our kids to improve while also communicating that they are wonderful and beloved no matter what. We can help them know that their worth is unconditional.

When children experience that unconditional acceptance, they incorporate it into their sense of self.

If your tension is rising as you think of the ways and times your love has looked conditional to your kids, please repeat this mantra: "I do good enough most of the time." Because while parents will inevitably sometimes give the wrong message, that's not what does the lasting damage. It is consistently judgmental, harsh, shaming, or fearful messages that create a lasting mindfuck from childhood.

OVERCOMPENSATING: PARENTING FROM GUILT

Tara brought her twelve-year-old daughter, Bella, in to talk with me about self-esteem. She did well in school, but she had a hard time with friends. She tried too hard to fit in and seemed to still feel left out. Home life revolved around Bella, but she didn't have many chores or responsibilities. Her parents had intense careers, and things were hectic with all of Bella's activities: dance, soccer, and volleyball. Bella expressed a desire to just hang out with her parents, but she was afraid to disappoint them if she asked to stop doing so many extracurriculars.

One day when Tara wanted to drop Bella off for her appointment with me so she could run to Target, I told Tara to hang on—the problem wasn't just Bella.

Parents and children alike are often overscheduled these days. Parents desperately want their children to have exposure and opportunities and personal growth. They are afraid to say no. The problem (well, one of the problems) is when too much activity makes it hard to connect and be present in the relationship without distraction. We are crazy busy, and we make our kids crazy busy in part to compensate for time not spent together.

In addition, children are so busy with activities that they don't know how to manage downtime. They don't learn to self-manage, self-soothe, and self-entertain. In some circumstances, kids aren't sure how to think without getting some direction.

For too many of us, life has become such a carnival that we don't know how to live without the insanity. As a psychologist, I strongly support giving everyone in the family opportunities for imagination, creativity, and stillness. *Especially* our developing children. I believe we are losing our children to a cultural phenomenon of always having something exciting going on—some kind of external stimulation (this includes electronics). The fear of missing out (FOMO) is causing us to miss out on real life.

I cringe when I hear of families who are always running to the next event, such as sports and lessons. I don't believe this is good for the kids, and I don't believe it's good for the family. Unfortunately, many parents see what other families are doing and they think, "I want my kid to have those opportunities. I don't want my kid to be different or feel left out." There is pressure to keep up, and it fuels the overcommitment we find ourselves fighting. We would be doing so much more for our kids if we protected their time to be still.

We need downtime too, and time with them. When we don't keep connecting—and it takes time and attention over the years—a hollow feeling of guilt grows in us. Scheduling more stuff is not the solution.

Settle Down and Build Team Spirit

For the next month or year (you choose the length of time), experiment with saying no to opportunities and activities for your kids. See that the world doesn't fall apart. What does happen as a result?

If these classic family-bonding moves are not yet part of your regular repertoire, try some: Make dinner together. Eat dinner together. Make meals an intentional time to catch up and see how things are going for everyone. When you speak to your child, let the communication go both ways. Have family meetings once a month to see what everyone has on their minds or to discuss what's come up, what people are worried about, and what acknowledgments, apologies, repairs, appreciations, and thanks need to be shared.

OVERPROTECTING: PARENTING FROM FEAR

Andy was a great father, dedicated to raising happy and healthy twins. Everyone was doing well. There were no major problems at home. Everyone felt loved. The kids got good grades and were involved in soccer and music lessons.

But then Andy noticed that as his kids turned sixteen, they were becoming more and more irritable and oppositional. He worried there

was something going on that they weren't telling him, so he brought them in for counseling. When Andy left the room, the twins exploded with complaints. Their dad was smothering them. They weren't able to make their own decisions, like, ever. They weren't allowed to go places with friends. They felt like their dad wouldn't leave them alone, and like they had no space. They especially hated his "third-degree" questioning style, which instantly made them want to rebel.

Andy was very loving. And his overprotective parenting style worked great—five or ten years ago. Now though? Nope.

While it is a problem when you don't provide unconditional love, it is also possible to love too much. That point comes when love is ruled by fear, and the parent overprotects. Yes, there are so many things from which we want to protect kids: drugs and alcohol, bullying, sex, danger, abuse. Then there are so many things we want for our children: health, a sense of belonging, enriching activities, good grades, and the like.

It's very easy to step into the trap of doing too much for and being too involved with your kids. In the end, we aren't doing them any favors when we overfunction and overparent. The point of parenting is to ensure that our kids will survive—that they have the skills to survive. When we do everything for them, we are not giving them those skills. We are, in fact, creating problems for someone else to manage—our future adult kids and their partners, colleagues, neighbors, and children.

Of course, there are real-life threats (like predators and terrorism), but there are times when we take it too far. We try and protect them from experiences they need for their own growth, such as anything that might hurt their feelings. Then once they leave the nest, our kids are ill-prepared for life, where feelings get hurt often. Life has complications, and it's the mistakes and defeats that create character and hardiness and grit.

#*@&*!!

No parent wants their children to face adversity (again, poverty, hunger, abuse, and neglect are too much adversity). In the past, parents couldn't help it to the degree that many of us can now.

Our job, as parents, is to make sure that we have exposed our children to real-life problems so that they can learn to solve them with our guidance. Then they are more ready to go out and independently face the world.

Guilty or Fearful Self-Talk

Does your negative self-talk around parenting tend to be more guilt focused or fear based? Or is it a fabulous combination of both? In your journal, list as many as you can of the most common scoldy, freaked-out things you say to yourself about your kids and your parenting.

From the work you've done so far in this book exploring your personality, core beliefs, and belief filters, where does all this shit come from? What conditions of worth (mistaken beliefs) did you learn as a child that might feed your self-talk?

Do you overcompensate? Do you overprotect? How and where does this show up? And how do you think this might be affecting your child's development?

Important: Be curious, mindful, and gentle about your answers to all these questions. Breathe. If you can't manage gentleness, sprinkle some salty talk on it, motherfucker. You're a crazy ass? Join the club, friend. There is a really broad spectrum of good-enough parenting, and no one is nailing it every time. *Do not* beat on yourself.

YOUR HEART IS A FUCKING LIAR

There is a concept that I teach my clients called "the head/heart split." It applies to a lot of areas in life, but it's really useful in child-rearing.

When you are in a circumstance where your head is telling you to do one thing and your heart is telling you to do another, always, always listen to your head. Your head will tell you the rational, logical truth based on facts and on your principles and values. Your heart will either tell you that your worst fears will come true or will offer you a wonderful fantasy.

Don't get me wrong: your heart tells you the truth about how you *feel.* But it lies like a motherfucker when it tells you what you should *do,* and why.

Acting on the guilt and fears of your heart will lead you to do too much for your kids, possibly stifling their growth. Instead, educate your head with facts about what a developing human needs, and make your parenting moves according to your values.

Say to your heart, "There will be pain. But there will not be suffering. *You must chill, motherfucker.*"

Some pain is essential to growth. When your child is going to do something or go somewhere new, she is apprehensive and begins to have second thoughts as the time nears. At the last minute, she wants to back out. Your heart says, "I shouldn't push her. She isn't ready. I'm going to step in and cancel." Your head says, "I should let her face the fear and conquer it. She'll be fine."

When we enable our kids to avoid facing their fears, it conveys the message that they are not strong. It also conveys the message that we don't believe in them. It keeps them from growing past fears and worries. Better to keep trying to find that sweet spot where we do protect our kids, but we don't smother them.

This involves a real MOMF moment for parents: we move on, motherfucker, past our own anxiety ("Is my kid going to be okay?"). And we enable the child to solve her own problems with guidance ("How can I help my kid learn independence?"). We don't just say,

#*@&*!!

"You're on your own." We coach: "You can do it!" It's all a learning experience.

GIVE YOURSELF A BREAK

When my kids were younger, I was a yeller. I'm not proud of it, but I've learned to own it without judgment. One day, when they were ages four and five, we were in a department store. They were both in the cart, each making the other more hyper. I was proud that I calmly said to both of them, "Don't make me go to the place where I am yelling, screaming, and going crazy." My oldest son looked puzzled for a moment. Then, he said, "Home, Mommy? Is that it? Is that the place?"

Busted.

Unfortunately, I tended to take their misbehavior personally. That was unfortunate, and I recognize that. I can recall times when I would be midstream yell and could simultaneously say to myself, "What are you doing? This is not good." Yet I think something about me enjoyed the release.

It's complicated.

I have, however, moved on—from the behavior and from blaming myself for it. What's done is done. I can say that I was justified, that I had to yell because they are boys, and the volume in the house just needed to be louder. I can also say that they don't seem bothered or damaged. I never yelled foul names or behaved in a demeaning manner. I just wish I hadn't taken their misbehavior personally. It wasn't anything against me. They just had other priorities. Who can blame them?

The yelling didn't make what I wanted happen any earlier or any better. I was just venting, and nothing really changed except that I became jacked up. When I notice my anger about the behavior of my child (like not turning in homework that was in his backpack), I take a

#*@&*!!

deep breath and have a rational conversation with him. I still discuss consequences, and the content is the same. The only thing that has changed is that I am not jacked up, and he is not jacked up in response.

Give yourself a break. You are not perfect. I am not perfect. None of us is perfect. The more you worry about doing things "just right," the more out of control things get. The challenges that face parents are hard enough without lopping on judgments and criticisms. You do the best you can with what you have at any given moment. Life is a shit show. Dance like you know the song.

In the context of parenting, MOMF is clutch. CBT, mindfulness, and a bunch of filthy backtalk help you do your work: on understanding why you do what you do, on noticing when you're doing it, and on letting it go.

Truth: You'll fuck up. You will commit unforced errors and hurt your child's feelings or her sense of self-worth. That's the **rupture**—it's the first arrow, and it *will* occur. This can set in motion two second arrows: one where you beat on yourself for what you did (note it, remember it, but move on—you'll do better next time), and the other where you don't **repair** things with your child. By owning your part of the problem, you show her how to take responsibility. And you give her a way to understand the issue properly: that it's not all about her, what she did wrong, how wrong and bad she is, etcetera. Kids can find some pretty intense conditions of worth in situations that seem minor to you. When you talk about the issue with calm and warmth and an even hand, there's less chance she'll go on believing some crazy shit she came up with in her amazing kid mind.

Take some care to do the repair thoughtfully. You likely don't have to apologize for everything you said—there probably was some relevant stuff in there. For instance, you don't have to back down on the issue of the child's misbehavior, if there was some, but maybe you do regret

#*@&*!!

what you said or how you said it. It can take some time to figure out where and how the repair should happen—tempers might need to cool, for example. But do it within a day if possible.

I'll leave you with a mindbender—the second rule of Parent Club (actually a pair of rules):

Rule 2a. You matter so much.

Rule 2b. It's not actually about you.

Both are true, and holding on to them both at the same time is *haaaaard.*

Bottom line: your kid's childhood is not your do-over or do-better. It's her life, and in a super basic way it's not about you, or your family, or your community's standards and expectations, or the economy, or the sad state of the world. It's about the love between you, and her drawing on that love to make her way in the world.

We all learn the job as we go. The ability to laugh at ourselves and move on to the next event in the feral cat rodeo of family life? That is a motherfucking lifesaver.

#*@&*!!

MOMF Like a Mofo

- **Calm yourself.** When you feel edgy and ready to lose it, take several, slow, deep breaths. Use some affirmations like "I am on my own journey. Each day is an adventure, and I will learn and grow. I am brave. Today, I will find peace, for I love my children."

- **Use counterstatements.** Remind yourself that there are always lessons to learn from the past, but there is no need to dwell there. Hold yourself accountable and use counterstatements (salty or not) to help yourself move on: "I won't be perfect. I can only do what I can do." "No sad stories today, motherfucker, because it will only lead to making a decision out of guilt. Guilt is the kryptonite that the kids use to get their way." "I'm listening to my head right now because my heart is a fucking liar."

#*@&*!!

CHAPTER 6

When Work Is a Shit Show

Cheryl came to see me because she was tired all the time, had no motivation, and felt downhearted. She wondered if she might be depressed, but the more she talked, the clearer it became that her symptoms were all related to her job. Cheryl worked long hours, including from home in the evenings after putting in a full day at the office. She felt not only unappreciated but actually despised by her boss.

This is a story I hear a lot.

These days a lot of people are expected to do more with less. But Cheryl's distress was more than just workload. It was about being treated like she didn't matter. Like she was less than human.

Cheryl's boss would publicly shame her team during conference calls. He liked to pit team members against each other. He said their low intelligence was why they underperformed.

One day, when he learned a project wouldn't meet its deadline, he started yelling and calling people idiots. He even threw his briefcase across the room. Cheryl felt like a hostage in a volatile and abusive situation.

Kids call it bullying. Adults call it being an asshole. Academics call it *workplace incivility*. Yes, it has been studied.

Michael Leiter,[12] professor at Acadia University, has written extensively about workplace incivility, which is rude or impolite behavior.

Leiter and his colleagues have evidence that workplace incivility leads to higher levels of stress and anxiety among workers. While incivility is plain rudeness, it can cross into abusive behavior, which is intentionally meant to harm another person's well-being. Abuse ranges from publicly belittling a person's work to name-calling to sexual harassment. The intent of abuse is to intimidate, humiliate, or otherwise harm another person or group.

Abuse is one of the signs of a toxic work situation but, as we'll explore here, it can be more subtle than that.

STUCK IN A SOUL-SUCKING SITUATION

Cheryl hated her job, but she needed the income. And she wasn't sure she could find something more bearable that would pay enough to support her family. This is a boat a lot of us spend a lot of time in—out there in a sea of bullshit without an oar.

To be clear, there are a lot of books, courses, articles, and podcasts about navigating a harsh work environment. And there's plenty you can do to build your personal brand or résumé, network, learn new skills, and so forth to boost your employability and make it more possible to make a move.

That's not what we're talking about here. Most of us can't just move on from a job. We've got commitments and responsibilities. We've got bills. We've got kids. There may not be a lot of employer choices where we live. We need the fucking health insurance benefits our soul-killing job provides.

So we're not talking about a situation that's not "the best fit" for you as a professional. We're talking about one in which your life, health, heart, and soul are on the line and you don't have a lot of real obvious choices. A situation in which you might feel dehumanized, anxious, angry, or afraid—and also stuck.

There are plenty of things you simply can't change about work. But maybe there are ways you are making it worse for yourself. We're here to get clear about the inside work you can do to protect yourself, be strong, have integrity, and be ready for your moment to (literally) move on, if and when it comes. While you're waiting for it to come, you can become a motherfucking master of MOMF.

Given the number of hours we spend at work, it's not surprising that workplace incivility and abuse (a.k.a. Working with Assholes) make us physically and emotionally sick.

But it's rarely just individual bosses or coworkers who make a workplace toxic. It's a culture thing, and it's everywhere you look. You know this if you have ever been in an uncivil or abusive workplace. You also know it if you work in a place where *everyone* has just given up. Where you know people have good ideas, but they keep them to themselves because they don't want to be disappointed or shot down again. At best, these workplaces feel like a spot you report to for a paycheck or parole, just hoping to get through the day without too much pain.

A toxic workplace can make you feel as if you're compromising your own values, and that is truly its own kind of hell. This happened to Ted, who told me that he loves mentoring younger workers and standing up for those who don't have a strong voice in the workplace. It's a thing he feels is one of his callings as a human being on this earth. More and more, though, he feels too unsafe himself to speak up for others. He has even thrown others under the bus once or twice. He realizes he is merely *trying to survive himself,* and it makes him feel like he is giving up on his core principles.

Let's talk about Cheryl a little more. And also Ted. And maybe you.

#*@&*!!

Though Cheryl has a very real need to support her family and her boss is a bastard, her self-talk is making her work situation more unbearable than it needs to be. Her self-talk, based on her unexamined core beliefs and belief filters, includes:

"No matter how hard I try, I can't get it right."

"It's my responsibility to make people happy."

"If I fight back, it'll just get worse."

"If I fight back, I'll get fired."

Ted's self-talk—again, based like all self-talk on his core beliefs and belief filters—is: "I'm such a failure." "I'm weak. Others need me to help them, and I am not strong enough to step up." "I even make it worse! I'm a coward."

Both Cheryl and Ted's self-talk is like their kryptonite. It loops and loops inside their heads, feeding itself, making it impossible for them to see the ways that they *do* have some power. They might not be able to do that awesome "take this job and shove it" move right now. But they can find ways to think and behave differently, and potentially feel better despite being up to their knees in assholes.

For any toxic self-talk, mindfulness and CBT are the weapons of choice. They'll take the air out of your crazy thought until it's just a sad little deflated balloon.

With mindfulness, notice the self-talk, and then challenge it with CBT ("What's the actual evidence for this statement?"). Do this whenever you can. When you can't, MOMF it up. Call yourself out on playing the motherfucker who is swallowing the poison being served up.

Take some time to figure out where pieces of toxic self-talk come from by looking at your core beliefs—these beliefs are why you believe your inner talk. Write about it. Fill in the details in some of your old stories that you maybe didn't even realize you were still telling yourself.

Both Cheryl and Ted might not feel safe to be their full selves at their jobs. But that doesn't mean that pieces of their best selves can't show up sometimes, when invited. And that, my friend, is not too shabby.

Are You Your Own Enemy?

When you think about your employment situation, do you tell yourself that you:

- Deserve the bad things that are happening at work?

- Have no control over the bad things that are happening at work?

- Can't make any real changes because of circumstances outside of work (people depending on you, bills, no other jobs available)?

- Are not good, smart, skilled, fill-in-the-blank enough to make any real changes about your work situation?

- Do not even have the first clue of what you can do aside from put your head down and keep going?

Take a look back at the exercises about your core beliefs and belief filters in chapter 1. Look for beliefs that you somehow deserve bad things or that you have no control. Where do those come from? What's the self-talk that happens inside your head when those beliefs get activated?

As I've said before, crappy self-talk is habitual, even automatic. And even at work. Build your MOMF skills for neutralizing it. For example:

- For each piece of negative self-talk, what actual evidence do you have for or against it? Then come up with a counterstatement that uses reason and evidence to defuse that habitual self-talk. These are your CBT skills at work.

- When that self-talk comes into your mind, try to just be curious about it. "Oh, there's that 'I'm worthless and my coworkers are going to find out' thing again. Why did that pop up just now? Am I hangry? Am I scared?" Flex your mindfulness muscles here.

- When that self-talk bubbles up, get salty with it. A simple, smiling "Bitch, please!" can do it. Or counter it with words *and* action: "Are you serious, brain? I'm going to go get a pedicure after work, because my feet aren't giving me any stupid bullshit. 'Worthless,' my sweet ass." MOMF skills put to use.

Working in Hell, with Assholes

Take some time to write about the pros and cons of your work environment, including coworkers, leaders, policies, pay, benefits, stability and job security, commute and location, industry, personal fit, and culture. Break it down. Do this mindfully over a period of time, if you like. Try to look at each aspect of the place, and of your place in it, with curiosity. Ask yourself: In what ways does [aspect of work] support my needs (like money, security, and personal safety) and my values (like honesty, service, learning, and growth)? In what ways does it damage them?

In what ways does [aspect of work] damage my health (including mental and spiritual health)? In what ways does it protect these? What do I find myself doing to try to protect these?

What are my work relationships like? Is there any ongoing incivility or abuse? Is there codependence (see chapter 4) or bad boundaries? Is there kindness and generosity? Are my coworkers professional and appropriate?

#*@&*!!

WHEN YOU ARE PART OF THE PROBLEM

I hate to say it, but it must be said: sometimes we're the asshole at work. Not because we're evil people, but just because we are trying to survive.

My counsel: Don't be an asshole. Instead, be a motherfucker. This involves calling yourself on your asshole ways. Do it with love.

Maybe start with putting some effort into telling the truth about how you find yourself doing shit that hurts your heart and soul.

Toxic Culture at Work

There are multiple paths to becoming abusive in the workplace. Sometimes it is a personality characteristic—a person is just a bully, and because the system is built for bullies or because they make up for their shittiness in other ways, they get away with it.

Sometimes it is learned behavior: most of us are not naturally dickheads. But maybe our supervisors are, or assholery and a hard heart feel like the only way we can manage to stay in the job. And so we adapt.

One time this tends to happen is during the critical period when we're being trained or otherwise learning the ropes of a new job or career. This happened to Michelle.

Michelle's Story

Michelle was a new social worker eager for more training after graduate school. She found a training program that looked fantastic. When she met her supervisor, she felt warmth and acceptance. She felt there was a good match between what she wanted and what the program offered, especially the promise of professional mentoring.

Initially, things were great. Michelle was an enthusiastic learner and she bonded well with other trainees. After a few

#*@&*!!

months, though, she started to see that her supervisor was coming to work late, leaving early, and pulling Michelle from training opportunities to do work the supervisor left undone. Her supervision meetings were canceled for no legitimate reason. Michelle started to feel like she was failing her own clients because she was unsure of treatment protocols. She became resentful of her supervisor. When she talked with the other trainees, they all felt this way, but they were too afraid to speak up, because speaking up resulted in being assigned more work as punishment.

When Michelle finally got the courage to bring up her concerns to her supervisor, she was told that she was lazy and had "personality issues." She was told she would get a reputation for being a complainer if this continued. Michelle was shocked. She had never heard feedback like this.

Sure enough, after this meeting, Michelle was "volunteered" to do extra on-call shifts. She was also assigned to do counseling with clients who had histories of sexual violence—cases that were beyond her experience and that felt dangerous. She began to feel demoralized and even afraid.

One day, a client became aggressive in a visit, and Michelle was threatened because safety protocols weren't enforced by the supervisor. Michelle brought it up during a staff meeting, and she put her concerns in writing.

Those were the right moves, right? Michelle was acting like a professional, in an organization that had structures and rules for the safety and protection of both therapists and clients.

Unfortunately, no. Michelle's supervisor told her to stop complaining and toughen up. She was "overreacting" and "being dramatic." The supervisor told Michelle that the field is a small one. It

#*@&*!!

would "be a shame" if word got out that Michelle was difficult to work with.

Because Michelle was a trainee, she didn't have a strong professional identity. She questioned herself deeply and finally concluded, "This is how training works. This is meant to make me stronger. It is tough love and for my own good so I can survive in this world of work."

These lessons taught Michelle to pull the same "tough love" moves on others when she became a supervisor. In time, she hardly remembered how wrong and unsafe these experiences had felt to her when she was going through them. When she did, she wrote them off as her being weak and naive.

Michelle's story is just one version of how a toxic culture can change a good worker in ways that she wouldn't have chosen, so that she becomes part of it. Based on her particular personality and on some of her core beliefs, she was inclined to interpret what happened to her as "tough love." She is an idealistic person with a big heart for helping people and good professional instincts. And she's now also someone who keeps a toxic (and even dangerous) work culture chugging along.

This sucks. And it makes sense that this happened to her, though it didn't actually have to. Most of her fellow trainees found other ways to cope: some of them burned out and left the agency; some burned farther out and left the profession. Some put their heads down and just tried to stay safe.

And some (like me, in the first chapter of this book) vented to their friends while they learned what they could about themselves and tried to find a healthier situation. That's the MOMF way.

So, yeah. Sometimes you are actually the asshole. Or one of them, anyway. It's a habit you got into because someone or something is really

#*@&*!!

unbearable, or pisses you off, or just pushes your buttons. Or everyone else is doing it, and you caught it like the flu. Now you react all over the place about people and things you might as well just move on from, because what you're doing is not helping anyone. Admitting that you're part (most? all?) of the problem is the first step to shrinking the problem.

Having integrity about our own side of crappy work relationships takes, well, work. It's easy to be resentful about the coworkers whose jackassery means we have to do the relationship work that they can't or won't do. Even if that work is just setting and maintaining boundaries, *it is work*. Extra work. Hard, not-fun work. But necessary-for-sanity work.

Are You an Asshole?

Jacked-up work relationships, and getting yourself right with them, is a good topic to journal about. Because this takes time and thought, and you are going to have lots of thoughts and feelings about it, the journal's a safe place to chart your path.

So go back to the exercise "Working in Hell, with Assholes." What did you write in response to the question, "What are my work relationships like?"

For each thing you wrote about a problematic work relationship, ask yourself, "What's my part in this?" and "Where do I have a choice in how to react to this?"

For example, if you wrote, "My supervisor doesn't know what he's doing, and he puts the blame on me when things go wrong," you might now write, "It might help him if I copied him on the report when I make a first draft. And frankly, during meetings, I actually don't know what I'm doing, either, and it feels terrifying. I'm going to consider how I might request some training in PowerPoint. I can also document when these awful presentations happen, so at least I have a record of my side of this. Maybe he is a jackass. But I do not have to make this about him, and how he's failing. I can do some constructive things that are just about the work and let go of reacting to his freak-outs."

#*@&*!!

Don't let it hang you up, and don't let them drag you in. Do it, and move on. When it comes up again (because, of course, it will), do it again, and move on. That's all.

GETTING UNSTUCK, EVEN IF YOU'RE STUCK IN PLACE (FOR NOW)

If you find yourself in a toxic workplace, there is hope of something better no matter what your circumstance. It will either involve some kind of shift in thinking (MOMF) or, if circumstances permit, literally moving on from a department, a company, a career path. In this world, there's a whole rainbow of possibilities between "Live your dream, you *star!*" and "Suck it up, snowflake. This is all you get."

For a lot of us, the question of leaving is not realistic due to finances or job availability. Those circumstances may change, but for right now it is what it is. If this is you, the first question to ask is, "What can I control?" There will be a variety of answers to this one, but the truest, best one is: Your reactions and your actions. Feelings? Not so much. Thoughts? With work, yes. Actions? Absolutely in your control.

When we're stuck in a job for now, it is important to emotionally MOMF. This is tricky. It involves being aware of abuses going on around us, calling them for what they are, recognizing how the abuses affect our self-talk, making a conscious choice to deflect as much abuse as we can, and letting go of trying to fix the toxicity. In other words, just because someone dumps shit on your doorstep doesn't mean that you should bring it in the house. While we can't control someone else's actions, we can control some of how we let it affect us. I admit that this is difficult and takes a lot of practice. And I promise it is still light-years better than the alternative, which is letting the bastards get us down.

When you work in a toxic situation, it is hard to not let it affect you. Willingly absorbing the incivility, toxicity, and abuse at work—and perpetuating it by beating yourself up with thoughts of "I should work harder, I'm not good enough, I'm not worthy"—is self-abuse. Telling yourself to "toughen up, stop caring, forget about it, fix it" is self-denial and dishonest. It is as if you are telling yourself that what you are experiencing isn't real, isn't bad, and (somehow, also!) is your problem to fix.

All of this is stabbing yourself with the second arrow. While there are times when you are clearly stuck, you owe yourself the honor and respect to call it for what it is—other people acting shitty.

Let Leaving Be a Possibility

Even if you think that leaving is impossible, it is important to spend time considering what the leaving scenario might look like. I worry that some people feel so mind-controlled by abusive behavior that they don't see options. Some feel so beaten down that they cannot believe there are any alternatives. For others, there really are no realistic alternatives at that moment. Still others find that change is hard. Playing out your leaving scenario on paper helps ensure you are seeing all sides. I am not talking about the win-the-lottery fantasy of leaving. I'm talking about making a plan to make a positive change, based on the facts of your situation.

Be mindful of negative self-talk such as, "I can't leave. What will I do? No one will hire me. I have to stick it out. People treat me this way because I am not worthy. This is just how it is. What if I go somewhere else and it is worse?" This is garbage, and just derails you before you even start. When it comes at you, force yourself to provide the evidence that these thoughts are true. If you say, "I can't afford to leave," ask yourself about *all* of the costs and benefits instead of just focusing on dollars.

#*@&*!!

Is the self-talk true, or is it *you* holding yourself back? I understand there are times when we may not have other job options. There are times when we need a certain income to support our families. It is still worth asking, "Should I leave this job?" Take the time and put in the work to discover what else is (or can become) possible for you.

Even if you can't change jobs immediately, you can make a plan for the future, which may provide some level of hope. There are also times when you may choose a lower-paying job or one with less status or less desirable hours in order to gain a sense of integrity. I am emphasizing choice and owning a choice, even if your options suck.

In *The Reality Slap: Finding Peace and Fulfillment When Life Hurts*,[17] Russ Harris talks about how terrible it can feel when we are faced with two bad choices. And yet, there is value in recognizing that we still have a choice, as it builds a sense of empowerment.

We *do* have a choice.

The choice may be between two undesirable options, but we get to make it. The problem is when we begin to feel that we are victims with no choice. We become resentful. If you choose to stay in a toxic work environment, at least for now, you need to MOMF past letting it eat you up. (This is *definitely* the scenario where some real down-and-dirty, laugh-your-ass-off MOMFing is called for.) If you choose to leave and make less money, you need to MOMF past being angry at lower pay. If you are honest with yourself and take stock of the situation, you can *own* the choice, be proactive, set goals, and focus on what you can control.

When It's Really, Really Bad

If you are being harassed or threatened, document it. There are legal consequences for those who break laws as well as for those who let

lawbreakers get away with it. If that's the kind of place you're in, document problems for your own protection and seek help from HR. In an imperfect world, help is not always where it's supposed to be, and seeking it may be really scary. Meanwhile, do your job to the best of your ability, don't be an asshole to other people, and put a high priority on moving on however you can.

Because staying in a toxic environment has the potential to cause short- and long-term health and psychological problems, it is important to put in extra time caring for yourself outside of work. Eat a healthy diet, exercise, and reach out to friends for support. As I have said previously, while talking about problems won't necessarily change the problems, it can help lighten the emotional load. As well, there is always the potential to see things differently as you talk aloud.

Make a Move-On Plan

In your journal, answer the following questions:

What would you like to change about your work? In reality, what can you control or do?

What negative beliefs and negative self-talk do you need to change?

Can you survive long-term in the current work environment?

If so, what will you commit to letting go?

What are your short- and long-term goals? Make a time line for your goals.

What first steps can you take today?

#*@&*!!

The best advice I have is to live in the present. Don't wait for things to change tomorrow when tomorrow may not come. Stop trying to fix everyone around you. Accept when things aren't under your control to fix. Don't waste talent. No matter what, don't accept other people's garbage as your own.

MOMF Like a Mofo

- **Keep a journal about significant experiences at work.** It can be good to look back and see what you have taken on as you struggle to understand how you are feeling. Sometimes we find ourselves in the pot of boiling water or taking much for granted. Journaling can help us see the bigger themes over time.

- **Write down your goals.** There is evidence to suggest that writing them down makes them more likely to happen. Keep a list in your wallet or purse or anywhere you can readily access. Even if you think you won't leave your job, it can be good to look at other jobs so you can make a conscious decision about what you really want. You never know what might come your way. Think of it as holding on to hope by making a road map for what you want.

- **Do something to counteract work toxicity.** Put something healthy back into your day. Eat healthy lunches at work, exercise, meet a friend after work, or do a positive visualization of you reaching your goals. Be vigilant of unhealthy coping—like emotional eating—which can also be self-abuse.

- **Create cuss-worthy counterstatements.** What salty MOMF statements can you develop to jar yourself out of patterns of negative self-talk and perhaps create a laugh at the insaneness around you? For example, "Fuck the poison." "Fuck the toxicity." "No way, motherfucker. You're not getting in my head!"

#*@&*!!

CHAPTER 7

When Your Body Betrays You

While we may be able to roll with it when life, work, or relationships fuck us over, it's a lot harder to stomach when it is our own body! It can feel as if a team member is stabbing us in the back. There are feelings of betrayal, especially if we work hard to be healthy.

When our health takes a nosedive, we may actually have evidence to support worry, and we may have reason for a pity party. At the same time, we can't let negative self-talk win. We have to dig deep and learn to cope with facts and feelings about our health. What choice do we have?

This chapter is for you if you are struggling with a serious health issue—an injury or illness or chronic condition that makes living in your body a challenge. Health challenges cut to the core of your identity. When physical changes have started dictating your choices in life, it feels raw. It feels disorienting.

Unlike some of the other issues we've talked about (work, relationships), you weren't in any way prepared for this. You sure as hell didn't choose it. But somehow it's what you have to adjust to. This is some hard-core existential shit.

Fear, sadness, anger, grief: these are all valid, legitimate feelings when your body betrays you. MOMF skills can help you put down the second arrow and stop yourself from making the moves that make things worse, from turning painful emotions into emotional suffering. MOMFing helps you see and accept the emotional quicksand, and learn to step around it.

In this chapter, we're going to concentrate on the second arrow of self-pity and victimization. I am not going to give you lifestyle advice. I'm going to give you some tools and perspectives that will help you cope with ill health—whether a diagnosis, a course of treatment, something chronic, something not treatable, or maybe something not even diagnosable.

Second Arrows and Your Health

Think about what second arrows you are stabbing yourself with around your health. Second arrows include self-pity, awfulizing, I can'ts, feelings of being victimized, what ifs, and hopelessness.

Take a few minutes (or as long as you want, really) to write about the hard feelings that come up around your health issue. For example, "I feel rage when I think about what that asshole drunk driver did to my leg." "I feel so much guilt about my pre-cancer diet. What if that's what made me sick?" Or "I am so, so sad that this is the body I have to live in now."

Acknowledge the feelings. They are valid and normal. Spend some time thinking about what you do with these feelings, though. Do you let them come and go, or do you ruminate? Do you let them discolor your mind by creating negative self-talk? Which feelings and thoughts are jamming you up? Ask yourself, "How is consciously focusing on these negative thoughts helpful?"

Catch yourself when you lock onto negative thoughts, and then visualize letting the thoughts and feelings go like balloons. What would your healthy self say to your struggling self?

How can you allow your real feelings while not letting them own you?

#*@&*!!

FIVE CHALLENGES TO FEELING BETTER

Many people have significant health challenges such as lung disease, heart disease, life-threatening cancer, and chronic pain. While individuals have a strong role to play regarding their health, there is a delicate balance between doing what you can and moving on, motherfucker.

In my experience in working with people around accepting and learning to live with chronic disease, I've identified five significant challenges people encounter: control, negative self-perception, anger, impatience, and hopelessness. The way in which we manage and resolve these challenges affects the way we cope and recover.

We'll be exploring how the five challenges have played a role in your health journey. We'll talk about how to apply CBT, mindfulness, and MOMF principles when you get stuck in unhealthy patterns that keep you from being your best.

Control: I Can't Do Anything!

When she was diagnosed with breast cancer, Bea was forty-four with a demanding full-time job and three school-age children. The diagnosis hit her like a freight train, and she was in shock. Bea just couldn't process how she could *manage* having cancer. She became preoccupied with the thought, "When am I going to have time to deal with this?!"

A world-champion planner and juggler, Bea threw herself into making detailed schedules and plans to cover all her responsibilities *and* her treatment. She coped with feeling overwhelmed by planning her own life and that of her family to the minute. Bea had always lived her life believing that "if I plan well enough, I can avoid problems." Her

#*@&*!!

self-talk was, "I have to get it all done. I don't want my life to be disrupted by cancer. I won't let it. I'll just work harder."

There was no room for error or for other people's limitations. Bea refused help from friends who offered, and she didn't let her husband take over home responsibilities because he wouldn't do things the way she liked them done. She had to be in control. It was all she knew to do.

So she began sleeping less, working harder to get everything done, cramming in medical appointments. Then one day she felt so sick that she couldn't follow through on her schedule for the day. That's when she lost her shit completely—and how she ended up coming to see me.

Bea and I identified her fear of the unknowns of cancer. Her what-if thinking was driving her to obsessive scheduling. Bea was trying to control what she could, which, in her mind, was "getting everything done" on time and to her standards. But instead of feeling in control, she felt like it was really cancer in control—like cancer was driving her bus, and driving her crazy. This was unacceptable to her, and it pushed her to the edge.

Really, her need to control was causing her to spin out of control. And she could see that, sort of, but what could she do? It was her best tool. Maybe her only one. And it made her feel strong (at least until it totally did not).

We started talking about using mindfulness and relaxation strategies to notice when she was falling into the control trap and to practice letting go. We worked on identifying her self-talk that demanded she be able to do it all on her own. Bea and I talked about how allowing others to help doesn't equal failure. It can be lots of other things, including a grace that we can give those who feel helpless, like our loved ones. We developed MOMF counterstatements to help her be more flexible, such as, "This shit show is not of my making." "Do I really *have to* do this shit right now?" "Let shit go, Bea." We chose affirmations to channel her frustration into energy, like: "Cancer picked the wrong bitch to mess with."

Using her expanded set of tools, Bea learned how to make a conscious decision to focus on what actually mattered. She learned to let go of things that she was doing just to get them done. When she had some what-if thinking, she brought herself back to today by saying some version of "I can only deal with what is right in front of me."

Not everyone plunged into a serious health condition reacts like Bea did, but control is always a factor. Sometimes we give up on thinking we can control *anything*, and this can be equally crazy-making. A lot of us (maybe most of us?) get a mix going: trying to control some of the things we can't (or control the things that aren't worth the effort to control) and giving up on some stuff we actually have the ability to change or at least cope with.

Even though we can't always control what we get, we can control what we do with what we've got. Unfair? Absolutely! But all we can do is the best we can with what we have. That part is on us.

What Are You Trying to Control?

When you think about control and the strong feelings it evokes relative to your health and illness, what things come to mind? What role does control play in your life? Are you obsessively googling stories and articles about your condition so you can understand 100 percent what's going on and what's going to happen? Are you trying to control other people's reactions to your health issue (rather than, say, ignoring them)? Are you getting into power struggles with your family or physicians about the best course of action? Are you pretending that nothing is happening?

Where do your efforts to control serve you and where are they hurting you, in your opinion? What CBT, mindfulness, and MOMF skills do you think

you can draw on to use (or develop) the helpful ones and drop the hurtful ones?

Spend some time writing about your worst fears. Describe what it would be like to acknowledge that there are many things that we just can't control.

It's a tender area, but getting the perspective of someone who cares about you can give you some valid insights into how you use control. Who can you ask? When you ask them, what do they say? And what's your response to what they say?

Negative Self-Perception: Who Am I Now?

When an illness or injury hits, it can play havoc with who we think we are. This is normal and understandable. But we have to find ways to adjust and move forward.

Ragen was twenty-five when we met. She came to see me right after she was diagnosed with multiple sclerosis. She was devastated. Prior to her diagnosis, she loved being active and outside—snowboarding, snowshoeing, skiing, waterskiing, hiking, rock climbing, snorkeling, you name it. Being newly married, Ragen had also been thinking of having children. She envisioned the "perfect" family of two kids and a dog.

Ragen took great pride in being fit. She didn't drink alcohol, smoke, or use drugs. She saw her doctor regularly. After MS, Ragen had a hard time getting out of bed in the morning because, as she said when we met, "What's the point?" It felt like MS had taken (or would eventually take) all the things she hoped for herself and valued the most about herself.

Ragen's diagnosis conflicted with her self-view. She saw herself as strong, accomplished, and healthy. Her body was a testament to her hard work and training. She believed that healthy behavior would result in excellent health and happiness. The MS diagnosis challenged all of that for her. To Ragen, the diagnosis meant frailty, weakness, and disability. Her self-talk became, "I am now sick and weak. Everything I've worked for is gone. My dreams are gone. Why get out of bed?" She was in a tailspin.

I started by asking Ragen to share what the diagnosis meant to her and to name her fears. Once she'd named her fears, we looked at how she was letting them scare her with worst-case scenarios for which she had no real evidence. Yes, the disease sucked and had real potential to cause suffering. However, it was not clear how it would present in her specifically. She needed to not get out in front of the facts by catastrophizing but to stay in the now, even with all its uncertainty. Mindfulness practices helped with this.

Ragen did grieve the loss of full health as she defined it, and through the grieving process she was able to reconnect with the strength that had helped her achieve so much of what she valued in life. We focused on the gap between how Ragen saw herself before the diagnosis and after. She became more able to hold herself accountable when she caught herself focusing on the negatives. She slowly readjusted from seeing herself as weak and unable, reinforcing that she was a person who was still strong but in different ways. Her self-view evolved—not from "strong person" to "weak person" but from "strong person with no health issues" to "strong person with MS." Her core self had not changed. Seeing and believing that made a big difference to her.

Sometimes—okay, a lot of the time—we're not lucky enough to get a clear diagnosis, or a prognosis, or a mapped-out treatment plan. Sometimes what's going on is so complicated and obscure that it defies doctors' ability to define it. There's no handle for everyone to hold on to, no map. Talk about crazy-making!

And too often that means that the people we most need help and support from—our doctors and our families—are skeptical about what's *really* going on with us. It's a lonely place. If this is what you're struggling

with, the work is the same: to get in touch with your core self—the self that the disease cannot change—and remember that *that* is who you are. No one else's ideas about you and your health issues can change that, either.

Are You Struggling with Your Self-Perception?

Is your health condition distorting your self-perception? When you got sick or injured, did your idea of who you are fall apart? Write about that, spilling out whatever you have to say. Then look at what you wrote and ask yourself:

Which of my core beliefs are making this harder for me than it needs to be? (Look back at the core belief work you did in chapter 1 if you want a refresher.) Write down those beliefs or belief filters.

What does the self-talk sound like? Write it down. How can you notice and talk back to these beliefs and the self-talk when they bubble up and make you suffer?

What is the core truth about yourself that this illness or injury can't touch? What can you do to remember that core truth when you need to?

Anger: Why Is This Happening to Me?

Odell was a hardworking thirty-five-year-old who was healthy until a car accident smashed him up. He came to see me after he'd already had multiple surgeries for crush injuries, broken bones, and nerve damage. The accident was months and months ago, and he was still not able to return to work due to pain.

Odell. Was. *Pissed.*

He had good reasons. First of all, the accident had not been his fault. Second, he didn't have enough money for the bills and was at risk of losing his house. And the insurance company was giving him the runaround. And his work was bugging him about returning. And his doctors gave him medicines, but they weren't working. Odell couldn't fish, work on the car, golf, get things done around the house, or do much of anything the way he used to do it. Everyone around him had an opinion, but no one had real solutions—just "a lot of noise and hassle," as he said to me.

Odell was referred to me by his primary care doctor because he had become "difficult." He refused to cooperate with treatment, he was irritable and moody, and he was losing his temper at home. His life seemed to be falling apart, and he was smacking down anyone who tried to help him.

When I met with Odell, I asked him about his "old" self. He was so passionate about it. He described an independent, tough, hardworking guy who did what needed to be done. Now, he said, he felt like he needed "a prescription to go to the bathroom." His *self-perception* had been turned on its head. He had lost *control* of his health, his finances, his independence, his work—his life as he knew it. Rage colored every thought he had. All of this, he said, was because some "idiot" driver hit him. He wanted the other driver to suffer, and he spent a good deal of time daydreaming about making this happen.

We identified one of Odell's core beliefs as "when bad things happen, someone is to blame." And it followed that that person at fault needed to suffer. And it sure as *hell* wasn't Odell. His obsessive self-talk was: "*I didn't do anything wrong. That asshole should lose his license forever. Why did he even have one to start with? It's not fair that my life is wrecked and his isn't. And none of these damn doctors are doing shit for me.*"

Odell's self-perception and sense of control were out of whack. It was all tangled up with his rage at the other driver and at his doctors and whoever else crossed him. The anger made him feel strong and energized, but it wasn't helping him cope. It was keeping him stuck. He

#*@&*!!

was worried and anxious about so many parts of his situation, and he wasn't addressing that worry and anxiety.

I worked with Odell to see where he could find some real control—while he couldn't change what happened, he could control how much poison he allowed to penetrate his mind. We discussed how the obsessive hatred was starting to destroy his family, and that he was actually making a *choice* to hold on to it.

Odell became determined to stop the avalanche of destruction in his life. When he felt anger, he decided to journal and do some physical therapy exercises. Odell also practiced deep breathing and visualization around letting go.

Odell decided that he could stab himself with the second arrow or say, "Fuck off, not going there today." I introduced Odell to *mindfulness-based stress reduction (MBSR)* as an effective way to reduce pain and let go of second arrows. MBSR is a very well-studied, effective program for managing chronic pain developed in the 1970s by Jon Kabat-Zinn. (It is offered free of charge online at https://palousemindfulness.com.)

Feeling anger in the face of pain is totally normal. It's even good and right! Anger is a powerful emotion, and it can make us feel some of that power, if only for a moment. Like with Odell, though, it can also keep us from moving on to the psychological healing we need to do around a health crisis.

Is Anger Keeping You Stuck?

Is anger a primary challenge for you? How has it helped you deal with your health issues? How might it be holding you back? Write it out. In situations where someone has hurt you, it can be helpful to write a letter to that person (that you do not send). It just helps you channel the emotion so that you can move on. If the person you need to write the letter to is yourself, do that.

#*@&*!!

And as you think about these questions, here's a tip: when anger comes with blame—either self-blame or blaming others—it might be blocking us from developing more sustainable, healthy coping mechanisms.

Impatience: This Is Never Going to End!

Farley was a forty-year-old firefighter when he lost the lower half of his right leg in a work-related incident. He was not going to be able to return to his old job, and when I met him he was suffering in his self-perception and a sense of loss of control over his life.

Not only that, but he'd also had to hire an attorney to help him with his worker's compensation claim. Like Odell, Farley was deeply angry. He had given his best years to his job, and now he felt betrayed by the city.

Farley loved firefighting, the adrenaline rush, and the sense of accomplishment that came from saving other people's homes and lives. He grieved the loss of all that. He also grieved the loss of camaraderie with his firefighting family. He tried to return to work just to hang out, but it wasn't the same. He was no longer part of the team, and he didn't fit in. He also suspected his former colleagues had been warned not to talk with him due to the worker's comp lawsuit, which was becoming contentious.

And he didn't feel like he fit in at home. He couldn't be the active father he wanted to be. He didn't like being supported by disability instead of a paycheck. He felt like a freeloader, a misfit, an outsider.

On top of it all, Farley had phantom limb pain—his lost lower leg ached terribly even though it wasn't there. Farley felt like he was losing his mind. He spent his days going to multiple therapies and doctor's appointments. What he really wanted to know is when it would all be over—the pain, the aimlessness, the appointments, the unemployment, the lawsuit. When would he be able to get on with his life?

#*@&*!!

Working with me, Farley identified his relevant core beliefs: "If you work hard, you won't have to worry." "Your worth is related to what you can do for others." "People who suck off the system are lazy." "You do what you have to do, and you own the results."

His self-talk was: "No matter what I do, I can't seem to make things better." "I'm basically a leech, worthless." "I'm so tired, and there is no end."

I taught him to counter his negative self-talk with "Fuck that!" It became his mantra.

Farley also needed to build some perspective so he could believe that change was possible for him. We discussed how bad it actually was right after the accident and tracked how much progress he'd made. He tended to gloss over this. As we spoke, he agreed that, yes, there would be "an end" to a lot of the circumstances he found himself in now. But no one could tell him when that would be. He had to find a way to let go of *needing to know* it.

How had he dealt with adversity and the unknowns of the past? I asked. He talked about this, then wrote about it so he would be able to remind himself when he felt swallowed up in uncertainty and darkness. We developed some spicy affirmations, including, "I've lived through serious shit, and I'm still standing." (Sometimes when he used this one he'd laugh and finish "I'm still standing—*on one leg, motherfuckers!*")

I asked him to keep a daily journal in which he could record his thoughts and feelings, track his progress, and check himself when he became convinced nothing was improving. Basically, he was learning to cultivate patience.

Finally, Farley benefited from doing some visualization exercises focused on him reaching goals. He visualized his strength and patience as that of a great big lightning-struck tree that was scarred but still strong and green.

#*@&*!!

Working on Your Patience

Patience is like a muscle. You have to work it to get it strong. Can you remember some times in your past when you have had patience in a tough situation? What did you do to access that patience? Where and how can you find patience now?

Look at your core beliefs. Can you find some that help you be patient with your situation?

Is there some self-talk that's not helping you see the bigger picture? What affirmations can you substitute for that negative self-talk?

Hopelessness: Why Bother Anymore?

Mitzi was a nurse who hurt her back while lifting a patient at work. When I first saw her, she had been off work for six months, having had lower back surgery. Her pain persisted despite physical therapy, pain medication, and consultations with rehabilitation and pain specialists. Most days, she rated her pain as an 8 or 9 out of 10. She passed her time moving from the bed to the couch trying to find a more comfortable spot.

Mitzi came to see me because she had become demoralized. She started to believe that her life was "over"—at age fifty. Prior to her injury, Mitzi was well-known in her health care system as a dedicated, caring nurse. She loved her job. She and her longtime partner enjoyed working outside, golfing, and hiking, and they were looking forward to traveling more now that the kids were out of the house. Now, Mitzi felt all of that was not just put on hold but lost. She'd gained weight and felt like a complete slug. She and her partner were beginning to argue.

Mitzi and I talked about how chronic pain is a disease. While I validated that her life had changed, I challenged her on her all-or-nothing thinking. Her line was, "Either my life returns to normal, or I've lost it all." We wrote down the negative self-talk that kept her from doing even

#*@&*!!

some of the things that she wanted, including, "Why bother? I can't do anything." And "Things will never get better. What's the point?"

As with Farley, I helped Mitzi grieve her real losses. And I challenged her to consider whether she actually could do some of the things she enjoyed. What were the things that were probably not coming back? And what were the things that might come back perhaps in a different form, or at a different speed, or with some mental and physical adjustments?

I posed one question that helped Mitzi a lot: Have you ever had a time when you were hungry but got so busy you forgot for a while? She had, of course. And it wasn't that that hunger went away. It is that she stopped paying attention to it. The brain is capable of something similar when it comes to pain. While we can't make the pain disappear, we can shift focus and we can give it less power over us. Would she rather have pain and be shut inside the house on the couch, or have pain while taking a beautiful walk outside? Put like that, Mitzi chose the walk.

I told Mitzi that research strongly suggests that enjoyable activities, within the confines of what she could do, could actually decrease her pain and improve her mood. I told her she could test it out, and she did. The results gave her a surge of hope.

Mitzi found that while, yes, she did have to give up some things, when she challenged her negative self-talk, it turned out she had a lot more choices than she thought. Simply scheduling activities that required her to be up and about distracted her from the pain, resulting in less pain and more joy.

The kind of hope I'm talking about is not a passive emotion. It's also not a naive wish for self-deluded people. It's deciding not to conclude, without trying first, that some things just aren't possible. Instead, it's remembering that we don't know what's possible until we try, and then being willing to actually try.

#*@&*!!

If you're someone who values certainty, hope can be hard to tolerate. Weirdly, it can feel better to just say, "It can't be—I'm sure of it" than to say, "Maybe it's possible. What's a good way for me to try it, and see if it *is* possible?"

When it comes to health and disease, there is much that is truly not fair, but the problem is getting stuck in struggles for control, negative self-perception, anger, a lack of patience, and hopelessness. At some point, in order to get as much healing as we can, we have to accept that while our health situation is a true motherfucker, we probably are too. We need to work through all our (totally understandable) bullshit and move on, with all the salt and sass we've got.

Finding Your Hope

What are your feelings around hope and your health? Do you need to feel certain, and is that need keeping you from knowing what to hope for?

Go back to the first chapter and look at the work you did there. What's your hopeless self-talk, and which of your core beliefs does it come from? How can you use MOMF to counter negative self-talk that terrorizes you with loss of hope? What MOMF affirmations can you use to remind yourself that hope is for the strong—those who want to live?

SECOND ARROWS CAUSE MORE SUFFERING

As you've worked through the last few pages, you may have noticed that the second arrow of health challenges stabs us when we let the confusion of who-am-I thinking, or the fear of what-if thinking, or the anger of why-me thinking take over our minds. More suffering is caused when we wake up in the middle of the night and hear our heart beating and obsess, "What if my heart isn't beating right? What if it stops?" More suffering happens when we wonder, "What if my cancer comes back?"

#*@&*!!

and try to make plans based on what isn't actually happening. More suffering takes place when we get stuck in thoughts of "This isn't fair!" "My life sucks." "I can't do this." "I don't want to have to do this!" "I should just give up."

Don't get me wrong. Like I said, fear, anger, grief, and sadness are all righteous feelings. And it's normal when health challenges bring them out. But when we let our fearful, angry, grieving self-talk *take over* is when we turn our pain into suffering.

Look back at what you wrote about in this chapter's exercises. Where are the second arrows, spinning you out into crazy town or keeping you stuck in suffering?

MOMFING DISEASE AND DISABILITY

There's a road we all take when we're dealing with loss of health and well-being. It's something like the well-known path for grieving other losses, a path that involves feeling denial, anger, and a need to bargain with the universe.

You've got to travel the road. There isn't a workable shortcut.

Feel It

The first step in MOMFing a big health event or situation (after accepting that it's happening) is letting yourself *feel*. It's perfectly fine if you say, "I hate this. I don't want it. I'm terrified and I want it to go away." Rage. Roll on the floor. Cry. Let it sink in.

The main MOMF skill in this stage is mindfulness. Notice what you're feeling without trying to change it. Name it: "That's rage." "This is fear." "This is guilt/shame/despair/confusion/sadness." None of your feelings are wrong. They get to exist. But likewise, none of them can be the boss. They don't get to run your life. That's not how you'll heal.

#*@&*!!

Reflect

The next step is reflecting on what this disease, injury, or damage means to you and for you. What do you think it means to have this issue? What are your specific fears? How does your health issue change how you see yourself or how others see you? How did this happen? How will this disease change your life? What will you do differently? What *won't* you do differently? How does all of this feel? How will you manage all of the emotions you feel? Write down answers to as many of these questions as you can.

It also helps to reflect on how your current situation measures up to past challenges. When I had cancer, it helped me to see the disease as an asshole fighting for control of my body. I'd growl at it, "You picked the wrong bitch, baby. You don't know who you're dealing with." I found that tapping into anger gave me more energy. It was a tool I really learned how to use by the time I survived that particular shit show. Ask yourself, "How did I manage other significant life struggles? What can I use from those experiences now?"

At this stage, get information from your health care providers and reputable books, articles, and websites. I do not encourage going to chat groups, where anyone can post anything. That can lead to feeling overwhelmed. Remember, it is one day at a time. Some days will be okay or even good. Some days will not. No need to judge it. Just note it and plan accordingly.

Accept Help and Love

Care from other people is essential when you get knocked down. That's why it's a core MOMF step. Determine who can give you help and love. Who will you be able to receive help and love from? And then call in the posse.

#*@&*!!

Take care: avoid talking to others who tell you what you "should" do (unless it's your doctor—that's her job) or who will bring drama. For instance, if your mom loves you but she's a lot of work, that's not helpful. Open some space between you. Stick with friends who listen and encourage realism and optimism. You want someone who will help you solve problems when you need it, but you also don't want someone jumping in to try to fix your life. You need someone who will help you face what's real and will move through this thing at your side.

Make Plans (and Plan for Uncertainty)

When you have a handle on what your emotions are and you have valid, clear medical information, it's time to make plans. This is another essential step. Start by asking yourself what things you can control and what things you cannot control. (You will ask yourself this over and over, because it will change.)

Here are some ideas to keep in mind when planning:

- You can (hopefully) control who you choose to lead your health care team and what kind of relationship you have with that person.

- You can control whether you accept help (even if you're not the kind of person who likes to accept help).

- You can control what substances you put into your body that may either help or worsen your situation.

- You can control whether you lock yourself up in a dark room or you stay in the land of the living where you belong.

- You cannot control whether a treatment works, or when and how much things will improve. In my experience, this is the hardest part for most people. We just want to *know* when things will get better. And we *can't* know it—no one can, 100 percent. It's…kind of a mindfuck.

Stay Flexible

You reflect. You understand. You accept. You do what you can to heal. Through it all, you keep on moving on, motherfucker. You make decisions, and you pick up the pieces if and when they don't pan out. You go about the business of living your life. You will have some good days. Enjoy those—*really* enjoy them.

You will have some bad days. On those days, look for patterns you might work on, and then be kind to yourself. Mindful practice helps you recognize that the bad days will pass. Moving on is understanding that everything is ever-changing, so there is no upside in getting too worked up. Things will change, again and again. Roll with it.

If your health, over your lifetime, is a book, what's the name of the chapter you're in? What has been written already? Where will you take the story next? No one knows what those future chapters will say. Not me. Not you doctor. Not your friends. Not you. That being said, you can sure as hell have a lot to say about kicking aging, diseases, and health challenges in the ass.

Deep breathing, mindful acceptance, relaxation, visualization, and letting go are your friends in a time of uncertainty. How can you build them into your coping regimen? Will MOMF talk be effective in keeping your health fears in check? If so, come up with some saucy, salty affirmations—or clapbacks—that will keep you laughing away the blues and moving forward.

#*@&*!!

MOMF Like a Mofo

- **Join a helpful support group.** They are considered helpful if they focus on problem solving and information sharing. If the group is just about sharing sad stories, it can fuck you up even more. You don't want to be feeling like, "Shut the fuck up. I can't take it anymore." You want to be in a group whose purpose is to keep you moving forward. You want an emotional enema, but you want to know how to pull it together. You can find all sorts of support groups that meet in person or online. Start with your local hospital's website. Then check with national organizations that advocate for the issue that concerns you.

- **Try mindfulness-based stress reduction (MBSR).** During a typical eight-week program, you will learn to use mindfulness, body awareness, nonjudgmental thought, and acceptance to transcend chronic pain. It's a way to retrain your brain in ways that don't erase pain but make it much more tolerable.

CHAPTER 8

When You've Got Bad Habits

Asha came to see me because she wanted to lose weight. She felt like shit. She didn't exercise. She ate a lot of fast food. She smoked. She asked me if I could hypnotize her and fix the problem that way.

Oh, my sweet summer child. If it were that easy I'd be rich, and everyone around me would be healthy and happy.

Maybe it's occurred to you that you have a habit or two you might want to change. Well, join the club! We are all creatures of habit, and as a sort of behavioral autopilot, habit is how we deal with our complicated lives. It's powerful. And as often as it saves our asses, it kicks them.

Sad but true. But also: not the end of the story—not by a mile.

In this chapter, I'm going to walk you through a particular set of strategies that health psychologists use to help people identify and overcome troublesome habits—things like smoking, overeating, and overspending. The model the strategies are based on is called the *transtheoretical model* and it works well with the MOMF skills you've been using: CBT, mindfulness, and moving on from life's bullshit. Buckle up and read on, because shit's about to get practical.

CHANGE IS FUCKING HARD

Starting with the obvious: change can be a ball buster. It's Everest. Sometimes, it's an avalanche on Everest. It's also a given: in this life, change will happen to us. The question is, how can we choose positive change? And how can we make it stick?

Psychologists have answers (no surprise). James Prochaska[13] and his colleagues developed the transtheoretical model, and it has five stages:

1. Precontemplation

2. Contemplation

3. Preparation

4. Action

5. Maintenance

Let's take them in order.

Precontemplation is when you don't think you have a problem. (Someone *else* may think you have a problem, but *you* don't.) In this stage, your self-talk might be, "Fuck it. I do what I do, and it's my business" or "Yeah, sure, whatever. That's the least of my worries." When you are in precontemplation, there are things that can move you to the next stage (like educating yourself), but since your line is that it's not a problem (or at least not *your* problem, or *much* of a problem), you don't really have much traction. There's a fair bit of denial happening here.

Contemplation is when you have started to think that you may have a problem, but you're not entirely convinced it's significant or worth dealing with. Maybe you get some routine lab tests back and all is not well; maybe you don't get a loan because your credit rating tanked. Your self-talk goes something like: "Oh, fuck. Maybe this *is* a problem." In the contemplation phase, you want to learn more about the size, shape, and importance of this maybe-problem.

#*@&*!!

Preparation is the stage when you fully admit that you have a particular problem. This typically happens once your emotions are aroused (you're afraid, angry, ashamed, guilty). You know the problem and can name it, and it has become something you know you need to address. Your self-talk in this third stage: "Fuck me. I need to fix this." You begin thinking about what you could change. When this stage is well developed, you start to make plans: what needs to change, and how, and when?

Action (stage 4) is when you are actually doing something. You've seen the problem, you own the problem, you have made a plan to change, and you are doing planned things to bring about change. You say to yourself, "Fuck this. I'm done letting this control me. I know what to do, and I'm doing it." Progress is made. Maybe you even meet your goal. You are a badass! Victory is yours! Take a lap!

Or, maybe not quite yet. There is a fifth stage, and if you don't go through it as seriously as you did the action stage, you will find your bad self pinballed back and bouncing between stages 3 and 4. If you are a human who has not been able to make a change stick (a.k.a. 99.98 percent of us), you've experienced this.

Maintenance is the fifth stage. Here, you have made a change *and* are actively using skills to maintain it. This is the part when most of us get tripped up. The work isn't done even if it looks like it's done; it always keeps going. Your self-talk goes something like, "Fuck me, *again*. Why can't I just be done?" Those old ways of doing things are still wired into your brain, and they are ready to step in when the new ways get boring or inconvenient or just *hard*. So you make a plan to maintain, and you work the plan. Maintenance is like continuing to go to the gym long after you have built the muscles you want. You use it or you lose it.

The thing I want you to know about this model of change is that there is no failure. (Self-talk: "Fuck that. 'No failure'? I can't *wait* to

#*@&*!!

hear this one.") By "no failure," I just mean this: if and when you aren't able to stick to your plan, you take a step back to an earlier stage. It isn't a wash. Maybe you need to learn more, change up your plan, or choose a more attainable goal to start with. You can take the opportunity to learn what went wrong and how to do things differently next time around. That part? That's where your MOMF skills come in handy.

Does Something Need to Change?

Make a list of the things that are most important to you, and put them in order of importance. These are your *values*. Does the way you are living your life match your values? Are your habits supporting you in embracing your values? If some aren't, what are they? If you like, you can include any habits or patterns *other people* think you should change but you're not convinced. (You'd be in stage 1, precontemplation, in this case.)

Where will you be in five or ten years if you don't change these habits or patterns? If you could pick just one habit change that could have a big impact on lining up your lifestyle with your values, what would it be?

SO WHAT HELPS PEOPLE CHANGE?

When therapists use the transtheoretical stages-of-change model, they start with a technique called *motivational interviewing* (MI). The researchers who developed MI were studying people with substance abuse issues, which is notoriously hard to beat. While there's no magic bullet to help people change overnight, MI has proven to be really useful in helping people move forward on their journey.

Here's how it works in therapy: Once a therapist identifies what stage of change a person is in, they begin asking questions to help that person reflect. For example, say the client is Naomi, who drinks too much and was mandated to alcohol treatment after a DUI. Naomi may spend some time bemoaning how unfair the situation is. She only had two drinks, she is unsure why her blood alcohol level was so high, she doesn't even drink that often, and so on.

Teagan, the therapist, senses some denial and identifies Naomi as being in precontemplation. Teagen nonjudgmentally acknowledges the crappiness of the situation Naomi finds herself in. But she also asks questions, like:

"What happens next for you?"

"What do you think the consequences will be?"

"What do you know about alcohol abuse?"

"Has anyone in your family had these issues?"

"How did it affect your family member?"

The point of the questions is just to get Naomi thinking, *not* to force or manipulate her into change. This is true at every stage of the process, from precontemplation through to maintenance. The client is making the choices—the interviewer/therapist is just there to keep the topic open and help her figure out what choices she might make.

Researchers have found that MI is useful for anyone who wants to make a change. I assume that if you are reading this chapter, you are at least contemplating a problem behavior. The exercises in this chapter will do the job that MI does in the therapy room: help you figure out what you want to do about the issue you've identified. I'll use the story of Andre to walk through the stages with you. (We'll start with stage 2, because stage 1, precontemplation, is the one where you are holed up in clueless la-la land and probably not reading this chapter anyway.)

Let's get to it.

Contemplation: What Needs to Change? Why Now?

In his estimation, Andre was seventy-five pounds overweight. He felt awful a lot of the time because he ate junk food and binged on beer with friends on the weekends. It wasn't that Andre was a slug—he played in a basketball league and he worked out a few times a week. He had a desk job, though, and through boredom, mostly, he mindlessly munched on pizza, chips, soda, and candy bars. On break, he'd go to the coffee shop for an iced cappuccino with extra whipped cream. It helped him stay focused (well, the coffee part did anyway). Andre's doctor told him that he needed to start blood pressure medication and that he was on the path to prediabetes.

At first, Andre was pissed. His self-talk was, "I've always eaten whatever I wanted. Fuck this. This is bullshit!" He wanted to know what had changed. Bodies change, of course. Andre's had, like everyone's. He had to get over the initial fear and shock, and that was the first thing we worked on in therapy.

I asked him where he would find himself in five years if he didn't make a change. I also asked him to make a list of things he valued in life and rank them. Health was high on his list. I then asked him to post that list where he could see it every day.

Once he had a little time to process the news from the doctor, he accepted that his ability to eat "whatever" had changed and that he needed to change along with it. Although he wondered what kind of masochistic bullshit he would have to endure to lose weight, he came up with some new self-talk to sub in for "What the hell?" He embraced "You can do this, dude. It is so you can live and not die of a heart attack." This process was Andre moving from precontemplation to contemplation.

Next, I asked Andre to make a list of pros and cons to weight loss. (Yes, there are cons: Junk food tastes good! His friends would give him shit for cutting back on beer. Needing to watch what he ate meant he wasn't invincible. And so on.) I told him to write it all down. He needed to be honest with himself so that he was ready for when his self-talk was, "WTF are you doing? This is bullshit! Eat what you want." If the pros outweighed the cons, Andre was probably ready to change. If the cons outweighed the pros, he was probably not yet ready. If they were pretty even, it might mean that he was still undecided or conflicted. Andre had a couple more pros than cons, and they were big ones. So he decided to take action.

Are You Ready?

Of all the times that you could have changed in the past, what has gotten you to the point of being ready to do something about it now? Why is today different from yesterday? And how ready are you, really?

Let's try two different methods to look at your readiness.

Gut Check

On a scale of 1 to 10, how important is it for you to reach your goal?

1   Fuck that!

3   Mmmph, ask me again later.

5   Would be good, I guess.

8   Better than a trip to Cali, TBH.

10 Hell *yes!*

Check your gut a few times over the course of a week. Does your number hold steady, or is it all over the place?

Pros and Cons

This is a way both to check how ready you are and to start your preparation for change.

Make a list of the pros and cons to changing your life and reaching your goal. Big or small, catch them all. You don't have to do it all in one shot—take a little time to think about it.

#*@&*!!

When you've got a list that feels pretty complete, weigh each pro and each con 1, 2, or 3 depending on how big a deal it is to you (1 = not a big issue, 3 = pretty important). For example:

PROS	RATING	CONS	RATING
better breath	1	I'm probably going to eat a lot and get fat if I can't smoke	1
save a ton of money	2	I'll be cranky as hell	2
no emphysema, yay!	3	I've tried this before and it's really, really hard; I don't think I can face it	3

If you find the pros as a group weigh about as much as the cons, you might not be ready.

What will it take to move you to the next stage of change in your process? What are your deal-breaking cons and how might you shift them? When will you be ready to do something about it?

Be curious when you take yourself through these questions, and be ready to laugh at your bullshit. No need to beat on yourself about it. Shame is overrated as a motivator. If you want to help yourself get more ready, keep reading, thinking, and gathering insight and mojo. Real habit change is something people often need to get closer to over time, not one and done. You've got this.

Preparation: Okay, It's Time. Now, How?

The next task is to drill down to the *measurable behaviors* that you want to change, and then describe those behaviors in detail. The focus is on you, and what you can and will do. Again, focus not on your thoughts or feelings but on your *behaviors*.

Andre looked at his weak spots (random mindless eating, no healthy choices available when he gets hungry, limitless beer when he feels like it, vending machine grazing, and dessert disguised as coffee). He listed the specific changes he needed to make to each in order to reach the goal of a seventy-five-pound weight loss over about a year and a half:

- Count calories with a goal of averaging two thousand per day over the course of each week. (Research[14] shows that tracking helps people lose weight and keep it off.)

- Make a protein smoothie for breakfast each morning, and pack a lunch and snacks consisting of fresh fruits, veggies, and plenty of protein.

- Eat vending machine food only in emergencies (and make sure "emergencies" are rare through planning) or when it fits in with the calorie count.

- Get regular coffee from the coffee shop, and don't put a lot of shit in it. Keep it within the count.

- Cut beer consumption way down: no more than a six-pack in a weekend, and yep, those calories count too.

I asked Andre to rate both his readiness to change on each of these behaviors and how confident he was in his ability to do each behavior. This would be something we would keep checking in about as long as the plan was in action. Motivation ebbs and flows, so monitoring it and talking about it are important.

#*@&*!!

Plan Your Behaviors

In a notebook, list the specific behaviors you need to change in order to reach your goal. Pair each of them with another specific behavior you will do instead. For example, if I want to improve blood pressure so I can get off medication:

- Cut out extra salt → Dump saltshakers.

- Develop new stress management skills → Do one relaxation exercise a day from Youtube.com.

- Increase physical activity → Take a thirty-minute walk five days a week.

Now rate your readiness to commit and belief in your ability to complete these behaviors above on a 1 to 10 scale, whereby 1 = "Magic 8-ball says 'ha ha ha,'" 5 = "This will be a struggle, but yeah," and 10 = "Kicking ass *and* taking names." Again, do this rating a few times over the course of a week. It's easy to be all fired up one day and made of fuckit the next.

Setting Goals

It's important to set clear, realistic goals. While it would be great to achieve your goals right away, it will also be super discouraging when it doesn't happen according to ambitious time lines. It is better to set a goal that is easily achievable and surprise yourself with better-than-expected outcomes than to be disappointed.

So when you set a time line for achieving your goals, don't set yourself up for failure. Be in it for the long run. If you have a large end goal (like Andre's, say), it can really help to set smaller goals along the way. Perhaps you have a daily goal, a weekly goal, or a monthly goal. It's sort of like running a race. You should have mile markers along the way so that you know you are on the right path and acknowledge the milestones you achieve. Smaller goals are also checkpoints—if you're not hitting them, how can you adjust your plan for better results?

Along with goals comes an important piece a lot of people forget: a reward system. Although much of this chapter is focused on learning from what went wrong when we fall off track, it is also important to reflect on what is going right. Do not move forward without rewarding yourself.

I urge you to set up a reward schedule prior to making a change. As with goals, there are two levels of rewards: short and long term. Short-term rewards give you positive reinforcement as you go. For example, perhaps you get a specialty coffee at the end of the day when you have gone without smoking. Or a pedicure at the end of a week when you didn't bite your nails.

Long-term rewards are like a promise to yourself for the end of the road. You might throw the money you would have spent on cigarettes into a jar; after a month, maybe you use the money to buy something you've had your eye on, or maybe you save up longer for a weekend trip or visit to the spa. The point is that you need to plan to give yourself a tangible reward beyond the reward of making a positive life change.

Treat Yourself Right

Write down your ultimate goal and the time line you've worked out for it. That's your destination. Now think of some possible shorter-term goals. The purpose of these is to give you wins along the way so you can keep going, so make them winnable! It's better to hit twenty little marks on the way to the final one than to set two big ones that are a stretch.

Now pair each goal—large and small—with a reward that is going to make you happy and keep you motivated.

#*@&*!!

When you get your goals and rewards mapped out, remember they are not written in stone. You'll learn things about yourself that will help you improve your plan.

Action: Ready, Set, Go

When Andre had a plan for behavior change, I told him to set a start date. "Don't rush," I said. "Choose the date based on the amount of time you think it will take to really do the prep work." I also suggested that he make a public announcement about his intention to change so he would feel accountable. (This isn't a must, but a lot of people find that an announcement helps them keep their boundaries with friends, family, and coworkers.)

While Andre was thinking about his change date, I helped him finish his planning. He'd obviously need to make some kind of menu plan, including grocery lists, to work within his two-thousand-calorie target and allow for some eating out. "Not being able to have pizza and wings" with his buddies was a big "con" for him, so his plan also needed to let him enjoy game nights.

He would also need to consider what would interfere with his plan: What would be the barriers to his success? What would be his triggers? And what's the difference between the two?

Barriers are the real-world circumstances that will get in the way of your success. For example, if you don't have healthy food on hand, you may scarf whatever's available or skip meals and go hangry. *Triggers* are personal land mines: the things that flip the fuckit switch in your brain, driving you to do an old behavior or ditch a new behavior. For example, you want to stop drinking, and going out to eat (or going to the ball game, or being bored and lonely on a Friday night) makes you want to order alcohol so bad that you're hanging onto the cliff edge with four fingernails.

#*@&*!!

Once Andre had sussed out his barriers, he could make specific plans to deal with them. For example, if he figured out that a long day at work (barrier) would destroy his tolerance for fruit and regular coffee, he might keep an extra protein bar (or a mini candy bar or single-serving bag of chocolate chip cookies) on hand for when he wants something sweet or needs to feel treated, just a little.

Triggers have more voltage than barriers, and they often need strategies that combine practicality and psychology. For example, if Andre knows that the weekend golf trip (trigger) will make it hard for him to stick to just a few beers, he might make a commitment to drinking one water for every beer so that his stomach will be fuller. He could also tell a close friend his plan and ask for help sticking to the limits he sets. He can take his journal in case he needs to unload his feelings and sort through them in a safe, private way. And he can record a couple of affirmations or coaching statements on his phone to listen to when he needs help staying on target, including, "I control my choices, and I'm stronger than this!"

Map Out Your Triggers and Barriers

What practical barriers will get in the way of your success on a normal daily basis? Think about your patterns and problem spots in the categories of home, work, school, family obligations, travel plans, and other routines. Are there any special events coming up you'll need to plan for?

What emotional triggers can you foresee? Think of people, places, and situations. Write down everything you can think of.

What strategies will help you defuse or avoid your triggers? (Hint: If they are super strong, avoiding them, at least for a while, is better.) Brainstorm a bunch of ideas.

Now go through your lists of barriers and triggers, and begin to pair them with solutions. Figure out at least one reasonable "I can swing this"

#*@&*!!

strategy for each barrier (and a backup, if you can think of one that makes sense) and two strategies (plus a backup or two) for each trigger.

THE SECOND ARROW: BELIEVING YOU'VE FAILED

The saying "No battle plan survives first contact with the enemy" is attributed to lots of famous generals (a Prussian field marshal named Helmuth von Moltke said it first). Another one: "Plans are nothing. Planning is everything." The point is: to succeed at something that's hard, you need to prepare. Also, accept that shit is going to happen.

So when you've made realistic plans and you're ready to commit, take a shot at change. At the same time, know you are probably going to experience disappointment—in your plan, in your choices, in yourself.

I am using the word "disappointment" on purpose. The word "fail" has such negative associations. And according to the transtheoretical model of change, "failure" isn't even possible. That's because when things don't go according to plan or you don't meet your goals, there is an opportunity to learn. As long as you are learning, you are not failing. You're getting stronger and smarter. And there's no such thing as perfection; there's only more practice.

People who practice mindfulness might put it this way: you can never go back to where you were, because you have had new experiences. You are changed just by trying to change. Each step along the way is not good or bad. It just is what it is.

When we have critical self-talk like, "See? You can't do this. It's too hard. You're not strong enough. You aren't worth changing. You suck!" it creates unnecessary psychological pain and makes it more likely that we'll struggle to make positive changes. Believing this self-talk is the second arrow. When you try to make big changes, you will have *plenty* of chances to practice putting it down.

It will feel bad enough if you disappoint yourself. Do you really need to grab the arrows of guilt, shame, and self-harm and start stabbing yourself? If you become overloaded with negative emotions and beat yourself up, you give up your chance to learn. The negative emotions will take over, and you'll spiral down or out. If you use mindfulness, trying to stay in the moment, you will have a better chance to remember that it is what it is: not "good" or "bad" but an opportunity to reflect.

How's That Working Out for You?

A week after you start your plan, go back and rate your adherence to each of your chosen behaviors on the same 1 to 10 scale, making notes about what happened to make things easier or harder (or impossible) at various times.

Look at each. What factors led you to give yourself the ratings that you did? Why weren't you a 10? Why weren't you a 1?

What barriers and triggers came up, and were you able to use strategies to counter them? Did you come up with any new strategies? Were there triggers or barriers you hadn't thought of before?

What second arrows or unhelpful self-talk did you notice during the week when trying these behaviors? Where does the self-talk come from (your belief filters/core beliefs), and what MOMF tools do you think you can use to keep it from short-circuiting your goals?

Keep paying attention to your plans and your progress toward your goals. Don't hesitate to modify tactics that aren't working, after you've given some thought (including journaling) to why they aren't.

And when you look down and find the second arrow in your hand, drop it!

I once read that life will present you with the same lessons over and over until you master them. I believe that. If you take a moment and

#*@&*!!

reflect and accept what is going on (rather than reject it as bad), you can learn *and* you can move on, motherfucker.

We have all said we will only eat a spoonful of ice cream or a bite of pizza, only to find ourselves eating half the container or half the pie, or both. What's done is done, but you can ask yourself, "What led me here? Was this a conscious decision?" If yes, own it. If not, why wasn't it? How can you increase your awareness? Be willing to learn and practice calmly picking yourself up, and you will get where you need to go.

Maintenance: Use It or Lose It

The practices of planning, journaling, mindfulness, and positive self-talk will keep serving you after you've achieved the change you want. Hear me: they are *every bit* as important during the maintenance stage as during the action stage. More so, even. Don't be one of the people who says, "Shit! Glad *that's* done!" and goes skipping off down the old road without a backward glance. That's not going to go well. Old habits never die, they just hibernate.

Your traits are your traits, and your core beliefs are your core beliefs—remember, these don't really go away. They have years and years of stories and interpretations (your belief filter) supporting them. What you have on your side is skill at seeing and countering them when they're being unhelpful. Skill needs practice. So keep it up.

When you've reached your goal, revise your plan to keep clear of the barriers and triggers that could wake them up.

If affirmations or coaching statements helped you reach your goal, they'll also be key in the maintenance phase (otherwise known as "the rest of your life"). If you're analog, get a stack of index cards and write coaching statements, mantras, and affirmations on each of them. Write quotes that make you laugh and move on. Write anything that will motivate you to keep going when you feel weak or low. If your phone is like part of your body, use voice memos, text notes, GIFs, or whatever does the job. Are there apps that can help you keep your values, your goals, and your strategies front and center every day? You bet.

The point is to generate the kinds of positive, energized thoughts and feelings that can shift your negative, self-defeating thoughts and feelings.

When you notice that you feel like you might backslide, or you feel down, write down the negative thoughts you're thinking: "I can't do this. I always fail. This is so hard." Then use the MOMF skills that feel right for the job. Writing this stuff down lets you see patterns in your thinking over time and helps you monitor your progress. It is also nice to be able to look back and read what you wrote on a good day as a reminder of why you are making a change.

MOMF Like a Mofo

- **Learn to surf your urges.** When you're craving a behavior you've changed, research shows that urges are like waves—they always, always pass on their own, and you don't need to do anything but keep them from knocking you down. How can you distract yourself and delay your reaction until the urge subsides? Hint: Moving your body, especially in the fresh air, is a powerful reset. So is deep breathing.

- **Do it again.** Now that you've succeeded at setting and meeting a tough goal, do it again. What do you want to achieve? What do you want to change? What do you need to do to get ready?

#*@&*!!

CHAPTER 9

When You Need to Move on from a Painful Past

Forty-year-old Maria came to see me saying she felt miserable.

Nothing had happened recently to cause her to feel this way. But in giving me a rundown of her history, it was clear that Maria's parents had failed her. Maria's father left her when she was four years old, and they had no contact. Her mom was an alcoholic and verbally abusive, though now sober. Her mom tried to show that she was sorry for how she behaved when Maria was a child, but she never all out apologized. They both just pretended that it was in the past.

For Maria, however, it wasn't in the past. She remained resentful of her mom even though they saw each other regularly. It was a love/hate relationship. It was clear that the lingering hurt and anger from the abuse haunted Maria and was likely related to her current unhappiness. She just didn't know how to fix it.

People ask me the hardest questions—the ones they, themselves, haven't been able to answer. Questions like: "Why did God take my child?" and "Why did my uncle molest me?" These questions are infinitely harder for me now that I am older. In my youthful arrogance, I probably tried to come up with answers. Age and experience have taught me that there are some things that have no answer.

When people like Maria ask me why they were abused, I ask them, "Even if we could come up with some sort of explanation, would it ever make sense? Would it ever be enough?" Similarly, when a parent loses a child to an accident or a terminal illness, what explanation could possibly ease the pain?

There are times when damaged people who lack the skills to provide healthy love and to parent appropriately have children. This is a tragic, unjust fact that explains plenty, although it provides no understanding or satisfaction. Life is full of heartbreak, and justice too rarely enters the equation.

How we get past all of this is even tougher to swallow because it requires that you do even more work to get over what was done to you in the first place. And, sorry to report, that work involves the F word.

Yeah, no, not that one. You know the one I mean.

FORGIVENESS FINDING PEACE

I don't often use the word *forgiveness* when I'm working with people struggling with painful pasts, particularly when abuse is involved or they've lost someone or something dear due to the action of another. Most people recoil from the word, and why wouldn't they? They see forgiveness as a grace you give to someone who has hurt you. What the fuck?! They don't want to give something so costly to someone who is so undeserving. The self-talk is, "That SOB deserves an ass-kicking, not my forgiveness! No way I'll give him the satisfaction."

But forgiveness is not about that SOB. It's about you, the hurt one.

This is because holding on to righteous anger always means holding yourself hostage at the same time. This is not acceptable. So a more palatable term I often use is *finding peace*. They might be two ways of saying the same thing, but "finding peace" sounds like a process you can control, a gift you give yourself.

And *that is* what I'm talking about.

Hurt List

What painful events from the past are you hanging on to? In your journal, write down as many as come to mind or as many as you like. Start each with "It hurt when/that" or "It hurts when I remember that/how" and finish with a phrase like "my girlfriend ghosted me" or "I got hit by my dad."

Once you've written down all you want to, take a look at the list. Are there some events that you have more or less forgiven, or found peace with? Are there some that you feel you will never forgive? Are there any that cause you to feel hurt all over again just thinking about them?

Now just notice what each event feels like for you. Put a check mark next to each one that feels resolved—or that at least doesn't make you feel ashamed, angry, or miserable anymore. Put an X next to the ones that don't feel resolved—the ones for which hurt still surges up in you.

You might notice that sometimes the hurtful event is something you did or something you blame yourself for. These are not necessarily the same thing! We'll talk about each of these a little later in the chapter.

Once you've made the list, close your journal and do something kind for yourself, such as calling a friend or taking a walk.

Forgiveness, or finding peace, is definitely a process. It occurs over time—sometimes a whole lifetime. How and when it happens is totally individual. However bad the hurt, and however long it takes, remember that forgiveness is always a way for you to reclaim your power and your wholeness.

And again, it's not about the sonofabitch who hurt you. If someone who is abused waits for the abuser to show remorse or atonement in order to find peace, it probably will never happen. Waiting means giving

#*@&*!!

up the control you have over your own happiness and healing. The transgressor, who may be a seriously damaged human being, may not ever have the capacity or insight necessary to apologize or take responsibility. And it may be that nothing that person could do would be enough anyway. Holding on to resentment is like taking a poison pill and expecting the transgressor to suffer.

Finding peace, however, is something you can do for yourself. It may not take away all the pain or the loss, but it can decrease it enough that you can move forward with your life.

I often encounter people being unable or unwilling to dedicate the energy it takes to find peace. The self-talk is, "It is too hard. I can't take it. I'm afraid I will lose my mind if I think about it. I shouldn't have to do this. I didn't cause the problem. This isn't fair."

I get it, I really do. It isn't fair that you are left to do the hard work when you didn't create the problem. But finding peace is a commitment not unlike exercise. You have to dedicate time to thinking and feeling and then sitting with your thoughts and feelings. It is painful, and the results aren't automatic. By the time we're grown-ups, though, we have all seen that plenty in life isn't fair. Sometimes we can move past the unfairness with no fucks given. Sometimes it cuts deep and we can't seem to let it go. But one thing I hope you've taken from this book so far is that we can always play the hand we're dealt.

Second Arrow: Holding on to the Hurt

If the first arrow of a painful past is being hurt or wronged by someone else, the second arrow is getting stuck in a quicksand of anger, loathing, and self-pity. It's the continued damage done by living in the past and allowing the past to dominate the present.

#*@&*!!

I say all of this with a strong sense of empathy and respect for the traumas people have endured. I am not saying that any of this is easy. To the contrary. Letting go of the second arrow is incredibly challenging. It takes time and a lot of work. (And in the case of complex or severe childhood trauma, it often requires sustained expert help. If that's you, my good friend, prioritize getting that help. You are 1,000 percent worth it.)

Even for less-severe hurts, the arrow may be deeply embedded and may need to be removed carefully. And, let me be clear: It is not about forgetting what happened. It is about not letting it—whatever "it" is for you—control you any longer.

What second arrows from past hurts are present in your life? What might it be like to let them go?

SOME TRUTHS ABOUT TRAUMA

Darius is twenty-eight years old. As a child, he was sexually abused by his uncle over the course of three years, starting when he was seven years old. Darius never told anyone: he was afraid. But also he was ashamed. The abuse left him feeling like he had a "dirty secret," and as he grew he had a hard time trusting others with that secret. These days, he's mostly able to avoid seeing this uncle, which is definitely for the best. But he is haunted. His life is burdened by a mixture of self-doubt, anger, hurt, and shame. Darius would like to put all of this in the past, but he doesn't know how.

What happened to Darius was wrong, wasn't his fault, and has had profound consequences in his life. Childhood abuse is a kind of severe trauma. *Psychological trauma* is, basically, our mental and emotional response to some event that distressed us deeply. Sometimes it's a response to a single event, sometimes it's a pattern or series of events.

What happens leaves its mark on us, shaping our outlook and behavior from that moment on.

There are ways to heal from trauma. For Darius, hope lies in his making a conscious effort to transcend the past. But "transcending" doesn't mean that the memories and feelings go away or stop mattering. It also doesn't mean that we absolve the abuser of responsibility. It means coming to terms with what happened in a way that lets us be more effective at keeping what happened in the past. It means learning not to allow anger and darkness to continue to hurt us. It doesn't mean forgetting but instead saying, "No more now. I will no longer let this be a focus in my life."

It also means recognizing the effect of the experience on how we are in the present so that we can know our worth, set limits with others, and self-protect when needed.

A caution: we should not try to move on before processing what happened to us—it won't work. Trauma can't be brushed aside. Trying that just worsens the trauma. Taking time to reflect on what occurred gives us valuable information and perspective, and can make us stronger and more resilient.

For Darius, being sexually abused at such a young age was a violation that contributed to his having a hard time learning boundaries. He had a hard time saying no to others. We explored this pattern together in the safe space of the therapy room. Understanding it didn't change his difficulty with boundaries, but it did help him have deeper insight and self-compassion.

Self-compassion is an effective antidote to the negative self-talk that can follow trauma. In healing from trauma, we reflect and seek to understand and even honor how the experience shaped us. And then (only then) we move on, because we become *able* to move on.

Dealing with trauma is a sensitive, tender place. So where does MOMF come in? Some may argue it's inappropriate to use the profanity piece of MOMF with adult survivors of abuse. I would say that it depends on the characteristics of that person. MOMF-style cussing and sass are not for those who will beat themselves up with profanity. It's always about using profanity to empower ourselves to *not* self-abuse. If you're going to hurt yourself with MOMF, it's not for you, and this is true across the board, whether you're healing from trauma or coping with a job that sucks.

WHAT IF I BLAME MYSELF?

Sometimes the hardest person to find peace with is yourself. This can be the case both when you actually did something that harmed another (more on that later) and when you were the person who was harmed. That's right: we blame ourselves for the bad things that happen to us. It happens *all the time.* For example, I might hold myself responsible for being raped because I "should have known" that the crowd I was with was shady. Or I might believe that my friend ghosted me because I'm "so needy."

We tell ourselves some version of these things:

"I should have known better. Why didn't I walk away?"

"This is all my fault."

"That proves that I am my own worst enemy."

"I must not want to succeed in life because I do such stupid things."

"I deserve to suffer."

#*@&*!!

I am here to say, on your behalf, fuck that noise. Just no. These statements are a) unhelpful and b) wrong. How do I know? Maybe you're thinking, "We haven't even met! I *am* to blame for the bad things that happened to me."

Here's how. One of the first things I learned in graduate school is that, as a rule, people are doing the best they can at any given time with what they have at that particular moment. Who we are now (people with the most up-to-date knowledge, information, and experience) look back and judge ourselves at a time when we didn't have that knowledge, information, and experience. It isn't fair. We were legitimately doing the best we could with what we had to work with. And the no-self-blame rule is categorically true if the bad thing happened when we were children.

If you blame yourself for bad things that happened to you, do this next exercise for some perspective.

Your Core Beliefs and Self-Blame

What's a bad thing that happened to you that you blame yourself for? Write it down. First, describe what happened, and second, transcribe your blaming self-talk around what happened. Turn back to the work you did identifying your core beliefs in chapter 1. With your core beliefs in mind, think about what information and experience were available to you when this bad thing happened.

For example, say you got involved with someone who was, in retrospect, bad news, and he broke your heart. And maybe also while you were together he said some shitty things about your mind, body, heart, or habits. Just a jerk. Did you, when you met, look at him and say, "Here's a judgmental asshole who's going to run right over me. Count me in!"? Or did your

#*@&*!!

belief filters show you someone who'd been hurt and therefore responds by lashing out, maybe someone you could love enough to heal his hurt? Older, wiser you may now know that he was *both* someone who'd been hurt and someone who also now hurts others—including you—making him seriously risky boyfriend material. And maybe, looking at your relationship with your own family and what they taught you about love, you can see where you got the urge to heal him.

When you look back at who you were when you made a choice and ended up getting hurt, what core beliefs were you working from? Try to sit mindfully with what you discover, noticing judging thoughts as they arise. It's just information, and you are continuing to learn. Back then, you were doing the best you could with what you had. (If it helps to use that as a mantra, do it!)

HOW TO FIND YOUR PEACE

There are as many paths to finding peace as there are people who want to find it. I have met folks who have no clue where to begin and those who already have a plan. Regardless of where you are, it is important to have appropriate expectations. The process isn't about waving a magic wand and it all goes away. Finding peace may be actively practicing letting go on a daily basis. It may be an everyday choice or affirmation until one day you notice that you aren't thinking about it so much anymore.

I suggest that you start with some sort of inventory of what happened. The inventory is a tool used in twelve-step recovery programs, and if you look under the hood, you'll find CBT and mindfulness. I'm not selling a twelve-step program, so here's a story about how an inventory might work in anyone's life.

#*@&*!!

Lee's Story

Lee had been dating Shelley for two years, and he was dedicated. He gave up a great job offer to stay with her. He spent a lot of time helping her get her life in order after her divorce. He bought her a new washer and dryer. He was her handyman around the house. Lee even stepped in to help Shelley parent her two kids. Lee was head over heels for Shelley, and he gave her his whole heart.

One day, out of the blue, Shelley told him it was over. She said she was seeing someone else, and she didn't want to see him or talk to him ever again. She was cold, seemingly an entirely different person to Lee. He begged her to reconsider. He offered to work harder to be the person she wanted. He suggested counseling. Shelley refused all of this and cut Lee from her life without hesitation. It seemed like she did this after he'd fixed all of her problems post-divorce. Lee was bewildered. He never expected this.

One year later, Lee was still feeling confused, angry, bitter, and unable to trust anyone else. He didn't feel able to move on without an explanation. I asked Lee to write down what wrongs he felt were done to him by Shelley. I also asked him to note the things for which he needed to forgive himself (e.g., red flags he'd ignored) so that he could begin to trust himself again. I asked Lee to write what he felt he had lost. I asked him to write what made him angry to this day and what he was holding on to from the past. I then asked him to write what it would take for him to get past all of this. Finally, I asked him what he needed to find peace around, and whether that was even possible in his view.

Sometimes merely identifying and honoring the losses and angers is enough. Other times, people need to take another step. For some, the next step is sharing it with a friend or family member. For others, the next step is an unsent letter to the person who hurt them. I know of one person who set fire to photos of someone who was abusive. I have had patients who wrote a letter tied to a helium-filled balloon to symbolize letting go. Some folks get tattoos. Some just quietly move on. In the end, the path to peace is not something I can prescribe. It's something each individual must figure out for themselves. The path to transcendence must be individually owned.

Often, people tell me they want to confront the person who hurt them. In this case, I ask what they hope to achieve. If they tell me they "want to hear," "want to show," or "want to know," I challenge them more. I strongly recommend that folks not confront the transgressor if hearing the other person say something specific is the objective, because doing so will often end in disappointment. That's because you're expressing a need for something from the other person, yet you don't know where that person is in their readiness to honestly address the situation and say or do the things you're wanting them to say or do. In other words, you're giving up control of your healing to the other person to handle—and that can go all kinds of wrong. You can end up in a situation where you can feel victimized all over again. Please protect your ass better than that.

On the other hand, if the goal is for you to say something and be done with it, that is a different situation. Still, what you say can't be intended to enlighten the offending party—that party may not be capable of enlightenment. To heal, you *must* get clear and stay clear about what's realistic for *you* to gain from the encounter. Ten times out of ten, this will be something within your own control, whether it's speaking your truth to someone's face and walking away, or doing something more symbolic like writing, then burning, a letter.

#*@&*!!

Inventory Practice

A lot of the time, intensive inventory work is best done with a partner. In twelve steps, it's done with a sponsor. For Lee, the work was done with me, his therapist. This exercise is for you to do on your own, so please don't choose to work on your deepest pain. Instead, look at the list you made earlier in this chapter. Try to find something that fits these traits:

- A single incident (not a pattern)

- Happened at least a year ago (so it's not fresh)

- Happened to you when you were grown (not a childhood trauma)

- It still hurts a lot when you think about it, but you're not over-whelmed or consumed by it

Got it? Okay. Now break out your journal. Write about the incident in a sentence or two.

Now, consider what needs to happen to let it go. What would it take? Write it out. Notice when you are banking on something you can't control, like the other person saying sorry. Notice when any negative self-talk comes up. Write this chatter down too, and gently argue with your self-talk using some MOMF talk when appropriate.

Once you feel as if you've come up with a plan that you believe will give you some closure—and it does *not* depend on getting or hearing anything from the person who hurt you—choose your time to put it in action.

Afterward, go back to your journal and write about what you did and how it felt. Was it what you expected?

Here are two things to keep in mind:

1. Feel free to pull in some help from a trusted friend at any point in this process, especially if you are having a hard time separating out what you need from what you wish you could get from the person who harmed you.

#*@&*!!

2. It's probably not going to feel all better right away. This is a process, and you may need to revise it if you discover other layers of gnarl beneath the first one. This is one of the many ways the human heart is unlike, say, a carburetor. Healing is not the same as fixing.

BUT WHAT IF I ACTUALLY AM TO BLAME?

There are times when we also need to find peace around the harms that we have done to other people. For example, if I was on my phone while driving and caused an accident that injured someone else, I would need to find peace around the fact that I was reckless and hurt that person.

The anguish caused by our own wrongdoing has a name: it's called *moral injury*. It's the effect on us when we've done something that goes against our most deeply held morals and principles. Basically, it's a kind of trauma that we suffer because of something we did. Psychologists who work with combat veterans, for example, talk about moral injury a lot.

How can you function if you believe that an enemy lives within you? How do you move forward in life with integrity if you have wounded your integrity? How do you take care of yourself if you don't believe you deserve to be taken care of?

In the case of moral injury, action may be needed—meaning, in order to move on, you may need to apologize or find some other way to try to make up for the damage you inflicted. If I were the texting driver who hurt someone, I would need to first feel the full weight of anguish to understand, learn, and grow. Once I'd processed that anguish some, it might be helpful for me to give talks at local schools about the dangers of distracted driving. Maybe I would apologize to the victim if the victim was open to hearing from me. But if I don't do anything but self-punish, stuck in my anguish, there is no possibility that anything positive can happen.

#*@&*!!

Whatever it was that you did, being lost in powerful feelings of shame, anger, and guilt doesn't do anything good after a certain point. This kind of pain is often something a person needs help to move past, whether from a psychologist or other therapist, or a spiritual advisor. Life after moral injury will never be the same, but it can be meaningful. And healing is possible.

Do I ever see individuals who just aren't able to find peace? Yes. Finding peace is a journey, and I am not graced enough to see people every step of the way. Furthermore, if someone decides that they want to hang on to anger and resentment, that is their right. Who am I to wrestle it away? I wouldn't want to do that even if I could. These folks have already had enough done to them.

I do ask this, however: Are you ready to put it—whatever it is—in the past? Are you ready to move into the present and transcend the ugliness? There is risk involved. Letting go of the past will require you to revisit it, will be painful, and will change you. The decision to move forward must be one that you own. In the end, you are a survivor. Honor that.

#*@&*!!

MOMF Like a Mofo

- **Continue to journal.** I strongly recommend that you spend some time honestly writing down what was done and how it was hurtful. If you need to forgive yourself, it can be helpful to look at a photo of yourself around the time you made the mistake. This can help you generate some self-compassion. Ask yourself if there is something you need to do to make up for your mistake, such as apologize to yourself or others, make amends, or contribute to a cause.

- **Write a letter.** An unsent letter to the person who hurt you may bring you some relief—and maybe even a lot of it. Some variations include writing a letter and then burning it, or turning the hurt into a poem or short story. The power move is in speaking your truth without inviting or allowing the other person to respond. All the control in the situation is yours, and that alone is healing.

- **Seek help from a qualified therapist.** If you can relate to the descriptions of complex or severe trauma (especially childhood trauma), or of moral injury, love yourself enough to get help from a therapist. Our collective bag of healing tricks is basically bottomless, and we are here for you.

#*@&*!!

Get Ready, Motherfucker, for the Life You Want

By this time, you've got the message that move on, motherfucker is about moving on from:

- The past
- Denial
- Self-criticism
- Self-sabotage
- Shame
- Whatever else brings you down and tears you up

You also know MOMF is not about running away. Instead, it's about being accountable to yourself—really seeing what is happening while it is happening, accepting its reality, reflecting on it, and making conscious decisions about it. Above all, MOMF is all about that moment when you need to stop stabbing yourself with the second arrow. It packages self-knowledge through CBT, self-acceptance through mindfulness, and the seriously salty self-love of someone who is going to claim their power and sense of humor, no matter how fucked up their situation.

BECAUSE THERE'S NO PILL FOR LIFE'S FUCKERY

MOMF is not a quick fix. No pill here. But it is a tool kit for working through whatever life throws your way. I've given you the basic tools (in chapter 1) and a lot of ways to use them in the chapters on relationships, work, parenting, and the rest.

And because life is life, you will always have new chances and new situations to practice the method. There is no *done* and no *there*. As you go, you'll gain in self-understanding and in your ability to manage negative emotions, sometimes easing them and sometimes truly feeling them in order to learn from them. (Remember in chapter 6 when we explored the possibility that you, in fact, are the asshole at work? That was fun! But when that's the case, it's good to know it so you can deal with it.)

When you understand yourself, accept yourself, and have the tools and skills to take on the inevitable highs and lows, you are ready to take all of you—the amazing, assholish, brilliant, dippy, generous, freaky, fucked-up, glorious, and unique ball of human realness that you are— and channel it into your best life.

BECAUSE LIFELONG GROWTH IS POSSIBLE

My final piece of advice to you? Make a road map for what you want in life. The road map is just a guide, but goals matter a lot. Early in life, we generally have goals like getting a driver's license, going to college, getting a job. At some point, too many of us stop setting goals, and we may even start to wonder what our purpose is in life. We may lose sight of what we want and what we enjoy. Approaching life from a positive perspective—"What do I want?"—will help you claim your life as your own. Don't let the focus fall on what you don't want (e.g., to be dependent, to work at a thankless job). This just leaves you with whatever is left over.

#*@&*!!

Hear me say: fuck that.

I believe that we are more likely to get what we want if we have some idea of what that is—and if we decide we're going to go for it. We need to envision ourselves achieving our goals. We can't just aim for "something better." It's got to be more specific.

Elite athletes do this when they visualize themselves making the shot or hitting the ball. You have to be able to see where you want the ball to go. Just hitting it isn't enough. You will feel doubt. When you catch the negative self-talk or what-if thinking, replace it with MOMF affirmations ("Motherfucker, you've survived some serious shit. You're ready. You've got this!"). If you change your goals along the way, kudos. Just keep them specific, and keep your eyes on that prize.

The bottom line is that working toward living the life you want means you're in it for the long haul. It is a real gift to be able to laugh along the way.

Your Road Map

How can you own all the parts of yourself and create a positive plan for your future?

What do you want? If you close your eyes and visualize yourself as successful, what does that look like?

What steps do you need to take to get you there?

What's holding you back? How can you MOMF it?

Write it all out—everything you can see that you want to head for, and everything you need to navigate to get there. Revisit your road map often. Use it to remind yourself, and revise the shit out of it when you need to.

BECAUSE YOU DESERVE A HAPPY LIFE

Yes, a *happy* life. You deserve it, and you can have it.

When I say "happy," I don't mean always smiling and loving life. It is not realistic to aspire to always being on top of the world. Happiness also isn't about smiling when you aren't feeling it, or not saying negative things. It isn't about being inauthentic. Happiness means being content given that you will have good and bad days.

Some people think that if they are content, they may become lazy or not motivated to continue with self-improvement. That is not what I'm talking about. Contentment is being happy with what you have and where you are when you are there. It does not negate having goals or a path to self-improvement. Happiness and contentment are about trying to be mindful about what you have and where you are right now while keeping an eye focused on where you're going.

Only when we accept the goods and bads (and there are always goods and bads) can we move forward with open eyes and an open heart.

We may get frustrated because it often seems that lots of bad things happen at once. I argue that lots of good stuff happens at once, too. We just pay more attention to the bad—and remember it longer. This is what it is like to live life. You know you're alive because of these rhythms. There are bad times when we feel lost. A laugh can help, and so can remembering that the bad will pass. Because it will.

Everyone has the potential to move on, motherfucker. We can move on from past hurt and regret, messed-up relationships, guilt and shame, codependency, drives to control, work toxicity, and distorted beliefs about the world and ourselves. Everyone has the potential to let go and become the person they want to be, to let go of the second arrows and self-create happiness. All it takes is mindful awareness, understanding, commitment, practice, and a healthy sense of humor.

Get ready, motherfucker. Your life awaits you.

#*@&*!!

Recommended Reading

Assertiveness

Harris, R., and S. Hayes. 2011. *The Confidence Gap*. Boston: Trumpeter.

Codependence

Beattie, M. 1992. *Codependent No More*. Center City, MN: Hazelden.

Cognitive Behavioral Therapy

Bourne, E. 2015. *The Anxiety and Phobia Workbook*. Oakland, CA: New Harbinger.

Burns, D. 1999. *The Feeling Good Handbook*. New York: Penguin.

Finding Peace

Albom, M. 1997. *Tuesdays with Morrie: An Old Man, a Young Man, and Life's Greatest Lesson*. New York: Doubleday.

Harris, R. 2012. *The Reality Slap. Finding Peace and Fulfillment When Life Hurts*. Oakland, CA: New Harbinger.

Kicking a Habit

Beck, J. 1998. *The Complete Beck Diet for Life: The 5-Stage Program for Permanent Weight Loss*. New York: Oxmoor.

Claiborn, J. 2001. *The Habit Change Workbook: How to Break Bad Habits and Form Good Ones*. Oakland, CA: New Harbinger.

Mindfulness

Harris, R., and S. Hayes. 2011. *The Happiness Trap*. Boston: Trumpeter.

Johnson, S. 1984. *The Precious Present*. New York: Doubleday.

Kabat-Zinn, J. 1990. *Full Catastrophe Living: Using the Wisdom of Your Body and Mind to Face Stress, Pain, and Illness.* New York: Bantam Books.

Kabat-Zinn, J. 2009. *Letting Everything Become Your Teacher: 100 Lessons in Mindfulness.* New York: Random House.

Parenting

Gottman, J., and J. Declaire. 1998. *Raising an Emotionally Intelligent Child: The Heart of Parenting.* New York: Fireside.

Wiseman, R. 2013. *Masterminds & Wingmen: Helping Our Boys Cope with Schoolyard Power, Locker-Room Tests, Girlfriends, and the New Rules of Boy World.* New York: Harmony.

Wiseman, R. 2015. *Queen Bees and Wannabees: Helping Your Daughter Survive Cliques, Gossip, Boys, and the New Realities of Girl World.* New York: Harmony.

Personality

Five-Factor Model (OCEAN): https://www.mindtools.com/pages/article/newCDV_22.htm

Myers-Briggs: https://www.myersbriggs.org/home.htm?bhcp=1

Relationships

Gottman, J., and N. Silver. 2015. *The Seven Principles for Making Marriage Work.* New York: Random House.

Shame

Brown, B. 2017. *Braving the Wilderness.* New York: Penguin.

Brown, B. 2010. *The Gifts of Imperfection.* Center City, MN: Hazelden.

#*@&*!!

Endnotes

1   Beck, A. 1976. *Cognitive Therapy and the Emotional Disorders*. New York: International Universities Press.

2   Kabat-Zinn, J. 1990. *Full Catastrophe Living: Using the Wisdom of Your Body and Mind to Face Stress, Pain, and Illness*. New York: Bantam Books.

3   Bergen, B. 2016. *What the F: What Swearing Reveals about Our Language, Our Brains, and Ourselves*. New York: Basic Books.

4   Jay, T. 2009. "The Utility and Ubiquity of Taboo Words." *Perspectives on Psychological Science* 4(2): 153–61.

5   Byrne, E. 2017. *Swearing Is Good for You*. New York: Norton.

6   Oczkewski, S. 2015. We Should Teach Medical Learners the Art of Humor. *Critical Care* 19: 222.

7   Lesser, E. (2004). *Broken Open: How Difficult Times Can Help Us Grow*. New York: Villard.

8   Costa, P. T., and R. R. McCrae. 1992. *Revised NEO Personality Inventory (NEO-PI-R) and NEO Five-Factor Inventory (NEO-FFI) Manual*. Odessa, FL: Psychological Assessment Resources.

9   Myers, I. B., M. H. McCaulley, N. L. Quenk, and A. L. Hammer. 1998. *MBTI Manual*. 3rd ed. Palo Also, CA. Consulting Psychologists Press.

10   Barks, C. 2004. *The Essential Rumi*. New York: HarperCollins

11   Rogers, C. 1961. *On Becoming a Person: A Therapist's View of Psychotherapy*. New York: Houghton Mifflin.

12   Leiter, M. P., A. Day, D. G. Oore, and H. K. Laschinger. 2012. "Getting Better and Staying Better: Incivility, Distress, and Job Attitudes One Year After Civility Intervention." *Journal of Occupational Health Psychology* 17(4): 425–34.

13   Prochaska, J. O., C. C. DiClemente, and J. C. Norcross. 1992. "In Search of How People Change: Applications to the Addictive Behaviors." *American Psychologist* 47: 1102–14.

14   Patel, M. L., C. M. Hopkins, T. L. Brooks, and G. G. Bennett. 2019. "Comparing Self-Monitoring Strategies for Weight Loss in a Smartphone App: Randomized Controlled Trial." *JMIR mHealth and uHealth* 7(2): e12209.

Acknowledgements

Thank you to my friends and family for accepting and encouraging my wild ideas and crazy sense of humor. You give me the courage to step out into the arena. Thank you to Ed Levy for your kindness, support, and wisdom when I needed it most. Enormous thanks to New Harbinger for taking a chance on me. I am especially grateful for New Harbinger's talented editorial staff—notably, Jennye Garibaldi for being my patient, gentle cheerleader, and Clancy Drake, who is an absolute genius with ideas and words. Most of all, I owe a huge thank you to everyone out there who has given me the privilege of hearing their stories. The crossing of our paths has changed my life.

Jodie Eckleberry-Hunt, PhD, ABPP, is a board-certified health psychologist who has been in professional practice for more than nineteen years. She lives in Michigan with her family, including the family treasure, Bacon—the dog prince.

Foreword writer **Emma Byrne, PhD**, is author of *Swearing is Good for You*. With a background in artificial intelligence and computational neuroscience, she is fascinated by the flexibility of the human brain.

MORE BOOKS *from*
NEW HARBINGER PUBLICATIONS

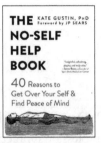

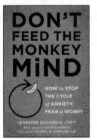

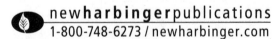